AN UNOBSTRUCTED
View *of the* Father

ON EARTH AND IN HEAVEN

RICHARD L. COCKMAN

Trilogy Christian Publishers
A Wholly Owned Subsidiary of Trinity Broadcasting Network
2442 Michelle Drive
Tustin, CA 92780

For information, address Trilogy Christian Publishing
Rights Department, 2442 Michelle Drive, Tustin, CA 92780.
Trilogy Christian Publishing/ TBN and colophon are trademarks of
Trinity Broadcasting Network.
For information about special discounts for bulk purchases, please
contact Trilogy Christian Publishing.

10 9 8 7 6 5 4 3 2 1
Library of Congress Cataloging-in-Publication Data is available.
ISBN 979-8-89333-953-6
ISBN (ebook) 979-8-89333-954-3

Dedication

This book is dedicated to my three very special daughters:

Malissa (Missy)

Rebekah (Boo)

Keturah (KK)

"I have no greater joy than to hear that my children are walking in truth" 3 John 1:4.

And to my wife, Malissa, who has selflessly joined and journeyed with me in ministry in Birmingham, AL., Arlington, TX., Lake Worth, FL., Midway, NC., Port Charlotte, FL., Duluth, GA., Fort Wayne, IN., and now Florence, AL.

Dr. Richard Cockman has written a book that is not only timely, but necessary. As he succinctly states in his preface, "Father absence is real." Then, he proceeds to offer a thorough treatise on the subject that expands in multiple directions from this basic premise. Beginning with a short, personal perspective from his roles as a son and a father himself, he offers a comparison of earthly fathers, who are human and fallible, with our Heavenly Father, who is divine and perfectly loving. With his education and decades of life experience as a pastor, counselor, and chaplain, Cockman is able to provide real-world scenarios designed to engage the reader. His insights are supported with examples drawn from the Bible throughout the book. The chapters are carefully thought out and well-presented, with discussion questions at the end of each that make it ideal for group or individual study. This work offers hope and encouragement as readers discover the delight of drawing closer to their Heavenly Father.

Laura G. Burger,
Writer and Copy Editor, Fort Wayne, Indiana

Having collaborated closely with Dr. Richard Cockman, I've witnessed his genuine care for others, extending to both the employees he served and his fellow chaplains. His extensive experience in biblical counseling, evident in his book, An Unobstructed View of the Father on Earth and in Heaven, emanates from a heart filled with Christian love and compassion. Dr. Cockman tackles the societal concern of absent fathers, drawing profound insights from his knowledge and personal experiences. I wholeheartedly recommend this book to individuals of any age or life stage who are deeply invested in the holistic development of children. Providing invaluable guidance for people across various stages of life, each chapter is meticulously crafted with real-world scenarios, drawing parallels between earthly fathers and our Heavenly Father, offering hope and encouragement. This book is not merely timely; it is an indispensable contribution to our collective well-being.

Dr. Kevin Bussey,
D.Min, M.Div., M.A., Professor
of Biblical Studies Highlands College

Preface

Being a dad is one of the greatest joys of my life. The influence a father has on his children and how this projects back to one's idea of Father God are real.

As a pastor, counselor, and chaplain in Christian ministry for 44 years, I have seen the void that is left when a father is absent from his children's life.

If you are choosing to read this book, there is a good chance your earthly father might have disappointed you. This may also mean you have a distrust, dislike, or disregard for your Heavenly Father. If you can relate to any "dad absence," if you are wondering if there is anyone who can truly be a redemptive father figure in your life, this book was written for you.

There is an epidemic spreading across America that is finally getting attention in the media. It is an epidemic of fatherlessness in our nation.

Father absence is real. It is not just the lack of a father's physical presence in the family, but also his emotional absence. This deficit can have dire consequences.

For some, their earthly father is completely out of the picture. He may have left his family by calamity or by choice. He sadly could have died. He also could have deserted his family for a number of reasons.

Whatever the reason for the loss of the earthly father in a family, some have transferred negative feelings over to their Heavenly Father, as if He deserted them. One might acknowledge God as a creator, but see Him as a distant deity that they have no personal relationship with.

The truth is that God is both our creator and our Heavenly Father. He has not deserted us but has provided a way back into a relationship with Him through His Son.

In this book we will talk about a perfect, ever present Heavenly Father and how we can draw closer to Him. We also will discuss an imperfect, earthly father, who is a work in process.

Introduction

by Missy von Herrmann, Daughter

The words of my father are more quotable to me than any movie line. His impact on my life has been that great.

When I was a child, I remember Dad would sometimes scoop me up and take me outside to gaze at the dark, night sky. Such moments with him were never planned, but to this day when I hear a choir of bugs after dusk, I am right back there with him.

I can still feel his embrace and smell his Old Spice cologne as he's holding me up with one arm and against his white t-shirt - the one he wore under his pastoral suit during the day. I can still hear him now as he points toward the expanse of a darkened universe and excitedly says:

"Do you see the stars?

Look!

There is the Little and Big Dipper!

Do you know who made them?"

Like the stars, though, during the day Dad had a way of disappearing on us around the house. It wasn't unlike him to suddenly get up out of his La-Z-Boy chair, leaving the television on full blast, head out the garage door (I can still hear the door shutting behind him), jump in his (whatever he was fixing up) vehicle, and take off toward that thing he needed to check off his list.

Being a runner like him, I often chased him down and would ask him, not knowing where he was going:

"Dad, can I come with you?"

Many days of my childhood were then spent under the hood of a car, following him down the aisle at a hardware store, visiting/praying with someone dying in hospice care, or stopping by church to check on something mundane that no one ever saw him fix but me. Wanting to be where my father was, and always being allowed to follow him, was a gift in my young life.

When I was sixteen and finally freed to date, I remember the words my dad gave to me before any young man came calling:

"BIG DAD will always be with you, even when *little dad* isn't around."

What a profound statement! It was an acknowledgement of my being cared for always, even when separated from the watch of my earthly father.

Then came the day I got married. Right before I was to exit with my new husband, I turned back to see my dad sitting alone in a chair with his head down. He'd taken care of me that day as he had all others - even walking me down the aisle, giving me away, standing on the stage to marry us, and emceeing our reception. That day, however, there was a finality in this role. He wasn't coming with me. He had handed me over to another.

Today, and after years of separation from him in miles, my dad has retired a short drive up the road from me. Now he is displaying for my children what he did for me - the valuable truths about life and God. He also loves his new name - *Pappaw*.

In this, it dawned on me recently to ask Dad if he had any regrets. I was surprised that he responded so quickly:

"I was never able to write a book."

(Of course, he later went on to assure me, as King Solomon reminds us in Ecclesiastes, that there is no end to book writing.)

However, one Sunday morning, I couldn't shake the thought of Dad's impact on my life. *What if I was to help him write a book?* As with any Godly conviction, my heart began to race and I started to listen.

I shouldn't have been surprised, but that morning church began with us singing, "This Is My Father's World." With a smile on my face and tears in my eyes, I knew it was time to allow both *little* and *BIG* dad to speak. This time Father God was holding us both close and pointing us toward His light.

"THIS IS MY FATHER'S WORLD"

This is my Father's world,
And to my list'ning ears
All nature sings, and round me rings
The music of the spheres.
This is my Father's world:
I rest me in the thought
Of rocks and trees, of skies and seas—
His hand the wonders wrought.

This is my Father's world:
The birds their carols raise,
The morning light, the lily white,
Declare their Maker's praise.
This is my Father's world:
He shines in all that's fair;
In the rustling grass I hear Him pass,
He speaks to me everywhere.

This is my Father's world:
Oh, let me ne'er forget
That though the wrong seems oft so strong,
God is the ruler yet.
This is my Father's world,
The battle is not done:
Jesus who died shall be satisfied,
And earth and Heav'n be one.

———

Missy von Herrmann
Florence, Alabama

Table of Contents

CHAPTER ONE:

Earthly Father/ Heavenly Father

EARTHLY FATHER

My earthly father's name was Herbert Eugene - or *Gene,* to those that knew him. My dad grew up on a small farm in the central region of North Carolina (between the Blue Ridge Mountains and the state's coastal outer banks) known as the Piedmont.

My dad's mother, Anna Kate, died of cancer when he was young and my Granddad George married a widow, Maude, who brought her children into the family. Two families became one large family with 19 children combined.

They all lived together in a typical homestead - a white house with an "L" shaped wrap-around porch. Inside there was a front living room where the nice furniture was kept for visitors, such as the small-town pastor. This room told a story, with pictures of family members in uniform who served in wartime, and artistic paintings of angelic cherubs.

The family room was more casual, with a pot belly stove (to keep warm) and a coffee can used as a spittoon for chewing tobacco. Down the hall the bedrooms were small and had no heat, so handmade quilts were used to cover up for warmth.

In the kitchen, meals were prepared on a cast iron wood stove. For a large family with many mouths to feed, this room was incredibly small. In the farming community, men would often eat first, then the children, and finally the women. Meals were composed of crops and livestock raised on the farm.

Farmers in that region and time loved their families, but were not openly verbal in expressing love. My dad never talked at length with me about his dad. Most demonstrations of love came through hard work and provision.

I remember my Grandad George as a portly man who always wore bib overalls. As a farmer, he plowed his land (of corn and a variety of vegetables) with two mules he named Ned and Jed. When I visited him as a child, he would sometimes say to me, *"Come here, boy!"* He was inviting me to come and sit on his knee. Without him saying anything, I felt a sense of security being near him.

Back then, and when someone died, the local funeral home supplied hand-held fans for the hot summer days. I jokingly remember thinking that when you fanned yourself you could see yourself "coming and going."

The graveyard at the country church near my family's farm holds name after name on the headstones of my relatives. Life really is a vapor, here today and gone tomorrow.

Although I am now in my seventies (and a Pappaw myself) I can still see, smell, and feel these details that formed my family. I do have a few fading memories of a man (Granddad George) who ultimately helped shape my father (Gene) who shaped me.

The father factor plays a significant role in forming who we are, how we think, and how we show emotions. So, when a father is absent in any way there are missing building blocks in the life of a child. Sadly, many today also do not have the privilege of a granddad's influence either.

How then are we to take an *UNOBSTRUCTED VIEW OF THE FATHER,* who has always been and will always be present in our lives?

HEAVENLY FATHER

Our Heavenly Father has no beginning and no end; He is eternal. Our Heavenly Father is not limited by time or space. Yet, much of our identity is wrapped up in our perception of who God is. Some (because of a limited understanding of God) have concluded He has little relevance in their lives.

The Bible emphasizes His relevance through relationship, not with many gods, but with one God - "Our Father." Calling Him Father does not lessen His status as sovereign God, but highlights His personal love for each of us. He has chosen to have a relationship with us, even if we choose to distance ourselves from Him. From the beginning, in the first book of Genesis, He came looking for Adam and Eve in the garden, even when they tried to hide from Him. In the same way He is still seeking us today in our hiding places.

It is God's Son, Jesus, who taught His disciples to pray in Matthew 6:9-13:

"Our Father in heaven,
hallowed be your name,
your kingdom come,
your will be done
on earth as it is in heaven.
Give us today our daily bread.
Forgive our debts,
as we also have forgiven our debtors.
And lead us not into temptation,
but deliver us from the evil one."

The depth of this relationship is not known until we choose to be united with the Father through a relationship with His Son.

God becomes visible to us through a look at His Son. While on earth, Jesus had many encounters with people where He was inviting them to get to know Him (and the Father) better, including this conversation with one of His disciples named Philip:

"Don't you know me, Philip, even after I have been among you such a long time? Anyone who has seen me has seen the Father. How can you say, 'show us the Father'"? (John 14:9).

Jesus is not a physical picture of God, but a visible reflection of the attributes of Father God. The love of Father God for His greatest creation, man, was evidenced throughout Jesus' earthly ministry. Jesus loved people, and demonstrated that love through both word and deed. The ultimate demonstration of His love was His death on a cross for humanity's sins. Sin's debt was paid in full on that Roman cross, and forgiveness is received through belief in the Son. Jesus put it quite succinctly when he said, "I tell you the truth, he who believes has everlasting life" (John 6:47).

Pagan gods require sacrifice, whereas our Heavenly Father provided the ultimate sacrifice for our sins through His Son. This gift comes from the Father's love for His crowning creation - man. This gift is not earned nor is it deserved, but is simply received.

FIRST EARTHLY FATHER

The first man and earthly father was Adam. He was created in the spiritual image or likeness of God. He was given the responsibility of caring for God's created order.

Some would say Adam is just another example of toxic manhood. Some males struggle today with personal identity because of the way men are portrayed on TV and in movies as incompetent. In contrast God said:

"Let us make man in our image, in our likeness, and let them rule over the fish of the sea and the birds of the air, over the livestock, over all the earth, and over all the creatures that move along the ground" (Genesis 1:26).

This is a reference to both male and female, who are creational equals. To demean one is to demean the other. Yet today's society seems set on pitting one sex against another, with the man being looked at in a lesser position.

What, then, is a man? He is a creation of God. He was placed on earth to obey the Heavenly Father, to work, to worship, to reproduce, and to protect his family.

THE FATHER'S IDENTITY AND INFLUENCE

Our self-identity is shaped through our understanding of who God is and how He is actively involved in our lives.

As A.W. Tozer wrote, *"We can never know who or what we are till we know at least something of what God is."* [1]

Charles Wesley, in the hymn "Arise my Soul." wrote: *"He owns me for His child; I can no longer fear, with confidence I now draw nigh, and Father Abba, Father, cry."*

Our earthly father is not infinite, but that does not lessen the fact of his great influence both in positive and negative ways in our lives. The Apostle Paul warns:

"Fathers, do not embitter your children, or they will become discouraged" (Colossians 3:21).

How have you suffered in the area of trying to please your earthly father, only to find a person who seemed unpleasable? Your earthly father was never pleased with your grades in school (he demanded A's when your best effort produced B's). Even your best efforts at perfection couldn't please him.

Maybe your earthly father wanted you to be a star athlete when your physique (that God gave you) was better suited for playing music, creating art, or working dutifully at a job. Even your best performance couldn't please him. Maybe you have always longed to hear words of affirmation from your father that have never been spoken.

There is a Father you can please. That Father is your Heavenly Father.

HOW CAN A HUMAN BEING PLEASE A PERFECT BEING?

Enoch pleased God by faith. In chapter eleven of the book of Hebrews, we see an all-star list of biblical figures who pleased the Heavenly Father by their faith and obedience. Verse six says:

"And without faith it is impossible to please God, because anyone who comes to him must believe that he exists and that He rewards those who earnestly seek him."

Faith is an acknowledgement that God exists, that He formed the universe. Faith involves trust and testing, which ultimately will be rewarded by our Heavenly Father.

The writer of Hebrews provides the definition of faith:

"Now faith is being sure of what we hope for and certain of what we do not see" (Hebrews 11:1).

So then, our BIG dad (Heavenly Father) and little dad (earthly father) must be regarded as different. Once you can do so, you can understand earthly fathers are not perfect, but are in process.

EARTHLY FATHER/HEAVENLY FATHER

Little Dad	Big Dad
Earthy father	Heavenly Father
Imperfect	Perfect
Dad is not God	God is God
Dad is dependent	God is independent
A dad comes and goes	God is ever present

DISCUSSION QUESTIONS

1. What do you know of your father's father? What was their relationship like (grandfather/father)?

2. What is the first thought that comes to your mind when you consider there being a Heavenly Father that created you, cares for you, and loves you (despite all your flaws, like Adam, that you have)?

3. How would you describe your earthly father? Do you see any reflection of him in you?

4. Do you believe that your relationship with your earthly father has affected your relationship with your Heavenly Father?

5. Did your earthly father ever encourage you? If so, how?

NOTES:

CHAPTER 2:

Earthly Father's Instruction

One of the roles of an earthly father is to instruct. I remember calling my dad weekly when I was serving with Corporate Chaplains of America. I was hoping to establish a closer relationship with him. Dad, coming out of a rural farming culture, held to the belief that love was demonstrated by providing and protecting. Love was not spoken but demonstrated. I strongly believe love needs to be spoken.

I would end our weekly phone conversations with "*I love you, Dad.*" There would be an awkward silence on the other end. I could have been defensive and concluded, "*If he is not going to speak love, neither am I.*"

Yet, I remained consistent until one day I heard him say, "*Son, I love you.*" It is hard to put into words the wave of soothing emotions that washed over me.

Men do think about speaking love, but getting it out of their mouths is a different story. I have jokingly shared that I just need to hit the back of my head with my hand to get those words out. *Why?* My family did not speak those words. Yet, that is no excuse for me to repress those important words to those that I love and to those that also love me.

It was not long after Dad spoke those words that he was diagnosed with Stage 4 pancreatic cancer. I continued to talk with him weekly on the phone and in one of those conversations, I asked him for some advice. Again, there was a pause and then these words followed, *"Son, I can no longer advise you."*

I felt the loss immediately. Dad was dying. Yet, I was thankful for the storehouse of knowledge I had received from him beforehand and the efforts I'd made to attempt to draw closer to him.

My recommendation to you, and as a son:

Ask questions while your dad is still here. Give him the opportunity to get to know you even if silence is all you receive in return. Speak the words, *"I love you,"* even if they are not reciprocated. This will free you in expressing love vocally to others.

HOW ARE EARTHLY FATHERS MADE?

When a child is born, an earthly father is born simultaneously. When I buy a new car, one of the first things I reach for is the car's manual. It's usually about an inch thick and covers everything you need to know about the vehicle. It would have been practical for have a manual when my firstborn entered this world as I really had no clue how to be a father.

My wife Malissa and I went through Lamaze childbirthing classes three times. However, nothing fully prepared us for the experience of childbirth. In labor, my gentle wife turned into a demanding drill sergeant.

When my firstborn was on the way, my mind was filled with a hundred questions. Yes, there are good books on the subject of being a dad, yet I came to realize that most of my knowledge on how to be a father had come from being fathered myself.

This made me wonder, *"Where did my dad get his understanding of fatherhood?* It was from *his* father's example. Truth be told:

Bad examples can travel down through the generations if positive changes are not made.

AN EARTHLY FATHER'S FLAWS

Over the years I have developed a technique I like to call "HELLO, GENE." You can try it too. (*Notice I am using my dad's first name here, so you can fill in your dad's name when trying out this approach.*) First, let me introduce you more to the character and nature of my dad.

Professionally, my dad cut hair in an antique-style barbershop (with a classic red, white, and blue pole out front) in Plantation, Florida. His shop was his calling.

In that community he was lovingly known as *"The Barber of Plantation."* This was a huge accomplishment for a poor North Carolinian boy, who as a young army soldier in WWII became a prisoner of war in Germany and was liberated to become a Purple Heart recipient. *(He carried a shrapnel scar from the war on his leg and a bullet graze on his head.)*

Outwardly, Dad had perfectly brushed white hair and a well-manicured white beard, which, against his slender build and jovial nature, made him perfect for the job. One of the strengths of someone who cuts hair for a living is that they become good listeners. Dad listened to so many for so long that he cut the hair of children's children. For some he became an adoptive father and grandfather.

Dad not only listened, but he gave great common-sense advice. He was a counselor without the certification. He had the ability to put people at ease.

32

BUT, like all fathers, my father had flaws. Yes, I picked up some good characteristics from Dad, but here is where the **"HELLO, GENE"** moments are obvious in my life.

I remember working with my dad in his yard in Plantation Acres, Florida. Dad was color blind, though I never heard him admit it. He was incredibly stubborn. He would argue with a stump.

That day I was trying to instruct him that the regular gas he was trying to put into his weed eater needed an oil and gasoline mixture. When the oil was added to the gasoline it would turn a different color, depending on the manufacturer. However, there was no way to convince him that he needed this mixture, so I said in one of my weaker moments, *"Put in what you want!"* I walked away knowing there would be no changing of his mind.

Similarly, there are moments in my life where I find myself repeating my father's stubborn streak. Like him, and in those situations, I am not willing to listen to good advice.

It is in those moments that I have this "light bulb moment" and say to myself, *"HELLO, GENE."* It's then that I can *choose* to carry on the stubborn streak or make a change. *(This is much like looking in a mirror these days, as I too now have white hair and a white beard, just like him.)*

TIP:

Rejoice in the positive, productive traits you have picked up from your father, but also be honest enough to admit that there are flaws you don't want to pass along to the next generation.

What are some of the negative issues that can carry over to the next generation?

1. *Addiction* - Drugs, alcohol, issues with food, finances, etc.

2. *Emotional withdrawal*- Suppressing issues instead of discussing them.

3. *Lack of love expressed* - Not speaking lovingly and vulnerably often.

4. *False affirmation* - Only being affirmed through accomplishments.

5. *Anger*- Expressed outwardly and/or repressed internally.

6. *Abuse* - Various types. All negative.

7. *Absence* - Not desiring to be fully present.

If someone has hurt or negatively influenced you, you have the power to release them from your pain list. Then you become a free agent. The key to opening old familial prison doors can begin with a simple prayer:

"Heavenly Father, I want to be free of this hurt and negative influence. I don't want to reproduce this in my children."

These generational curses can be broken, but you must have your Heavenly Father's help to determine that it stops with you. Forgive your father. Recognize he was most likely reproducing what he experienced. In this same way, you will be able to forgive yourself when you have those disappointing "old dad" moments. Of course, you could have a great dad and choose to reject his example and advice. We are not responsible for the negative actions of our ancestors, but we do have the power to influence our descendants in a positive way.

EARTHLY FATHER AS PROVIDER

Once, when I was talking with a financial manager in a car dealership, I asked him if the long hours his job demanded affected his home life. He admitted to the obvious time deficit with his family, but shared he was able to provide his wife and children with nice cars. He then proceeded to recite to me the years, makes, and models of their vehicles. He justified his lack of time with his family with the substitute of things.

Men are taught that if you want to be a *good father* then you need to be a *good provider*. Certainly, providing isn't a bad thing in itself. However, provision is not just about being able to supply food, shelter and transportation. Being a provider is a much wider responsibility.

What adult *(looking back on their childhood)* would be willing to trade *things* for *more time* with their dad?

Sure, the money your dad stuck in your pocket was appreciated, but what about a big, priceless hug and the words every child longs to hear:

"*(Insert your name here), Dad loves you and is so proud of you.*"

(*Notice: Here, Dad didn't say, "I am proud of what you have done," but he affirmed the child for simply being his.*)

Some children grow up to spend their lives trying to gain their earthly father's approval. Remember: the love of our Heavenly Father is not based on what we do, but who we are in relationship with Him through His Son.

This relationship is established by what is called "*saving faith.*" Saving faith is simply the transfer of our trust to what God has declared. It is not just an intellectual assent, but a soul assent.

It is trusting Jesus alone for an eternal life and a heavenly home with God the Father, Jesus the Son, and the Holy Spirit. I like to say we turn from doing our own thing to demonstrating our love for God through obedience.

FATHER AS PROTECTOR

"In a sense, any responsible man serves as the tip of his own family's spear. A woman provides essential support, but it is the man whose essential duty is to protect his loved ones from harm."[2]

This was re-emphasized to me in the early days of marriage.

I remember Malissa and me, in our first apartment, crawling into our bed for a night's rest. This was a unique bed in the fact that no matter where you lay on the bed you would end up in the middle. It reminded me of a sway-backed horse. As we began to settle in, I heard my young bride trying to hold back tears. Since I came from a counseling background, I thought it might be wise to ask the question:

"What's wrong, honey?"

I was caught off guard when she whimpered:

"You...didn't...check...the door...
Dad always checked the door."

The role of protector had now passed from father to husband. Protection is not just just locking the door. Yes, it's providing physical safety, but it is also much more. Forces and influencers abound that can hurt our children emotionally and spiritually.

As a protector it might be a good idea to set limits on media exposure, and to know what your children are watching and listening to. Don't be in a hurry to put that cell phone in their hands.

EARTHLY FATHER AS AN EXAMPLE

Children tend to follow what they see rather than what they are told. A dad can tell his son, *"You need to go to church with your mom."* However, if a dad doesn't provide this example and stays home on Sundays, when his son reaches a certain age, he is prone to follow his dad's lead. So then, the son's rationalization instinctively becomes, *"Why should I go to church? Dad doesn't."*

A pivotal moment in my teenage life was when I was living with my parents and my younger brother Tim in a small duplex in Lauderhill, Florida. At the time, and during my high school years, I was struggling with my relationship with my Heavenly Father because I wanted to do my own thing and not be subject to any higher authority.

My brother Tim and I slept in a very small bedroom. One night I remember seeing light coming from our cracked bedroom door. As I quietly peered through the crack, and in the middle of the night, I saw my dad sitting on the couch reading his Bible and spending time with his Heavenly Father. He didn't have to tell me, *"Read your Bible and pray."* I literally saw my Dad doing exactly that -

communing with his Heavenly Father. That moment spoke a thousand words to my heart through his example.

Before Missy, my firstborn, could understand exactly what I was teaching her, I knew the importance of taking her in my arms and talking to her. When she was very young, and while we were living in Arlington, Texas, I vividly recall taking her in my arms and going outside to show her a rainbow. I didn't go into a scientific explanation, but in a gentle voice, pointing to the rainbow in the sky said, *"Honey, look! God made that, and in the rainbow, there is a promise."* I don't know if she remembers that moment in time, but she heard my voice and felt the safety of my arms.

Missy, and all my daughters, slept in my childhood crib as babies, which I always thought was very special. Nightly, I would put my hands on their heads and pray for them there.

One night, when Missy was big enough to pull up on the rails, I forgot to put my hands on her head while I was praying. With my eyes closed I felt her tiny hands take my hands and place them on her head. It was not only the voice she took comfort in, but my touch. Touch can provide healing and security too.

What you do today can make a lasting impact. Take reading to your children as an example. In our small parsonage in Lake Worth, Florida I remember reading *The Chronicles of Narnia* by C.S. Lewis to my girls. I'm sure they didn't understand all of the Biblical analogies in the stories at the time. Yet, I am confident (as they are all now believers in Jesus) that they grew to understand who Aslan represented.

As you read and pray, your children will learn through your example. Make the effort. They will someday credit you for it.

FATHER AND FAMILY

I believe the family is the superglue that holds any society together. With the demise of society, the family has suffered. Today there is a growing clash between family values and the societal drift from traditional values we once held as sacred. Absolutes are being replaced with the shifting sands of relativism.

A father must realize that his greatest accomplishments in life will be in helping his children to establish principles and values. Being a financial provider is only one part of fatherhood. Family is an investment in future fathers, future mothers, and future world changers.

Dad, it is also important to have dinner together as a family. Ronald Reagan in his farewell message to the nation on January 11, 1989 shared:

"And let me offer lesson number one about America: All great change in America begins at the dinner table."

At the dinner table we experience the cohesion of the family, that sense of togetherness. It is a time to catch up on what the day held. It is a place to offer support and encouragement. It is a place to reinforce values, beliefs, and principles. It is a place to talk. It is a place to listen.

WHAT ARE SOME CHARACTERISTICS OF A HEALTHY FAMILY?

1. A father and mother are present (best case scenario).

2. The members value one another.

3. Love is spoken.

4. They laugh together.

5. Touch is meaningful.

6. They listen to one another.

7. They have household routines (such as nightly meals together).

8. They celebrate each other's accomplishments.

9. Together is a safe place to be.

10. They enjoy activities together outside of the home.

WHAT ARE SOME CHARACTERISTICS OF AN UNHEALTHY FAMILY?

1. Absence of one (or both) parents.

2. Members are self-centered.

3. Love is not spoken.

4. Laughter at the expense of another.

5. Abuse is present.

6. Lack of cohesiveness.

7. When together, fear is present.

8. Disappointment is a theme.

9. The household feels controlling and combative.

10. Anger is rampant - inside and outside of the home.

A WARNING FOR FATHERS AND CHILDREN IN A FALTERING SOCIETY

Today I am hearing through the media and public educators the words *"our children."* This concerns me.

In socialism, the family becomes the responsibility of the state. Instead of seeing the nuclear/extended family as the caregiver of children and grandchildren, the state becomes the substitute. The state becomes the influencer of "our children" from cradle to the grave. When this happens, loyalty to the family can be surrendered for loyalty to the state. Socialism breeds Epicureanism, or a focus on self and personal pleasure.

"Many Epicurean fans these days want to insist that mother and fathers are interchangeable or better replaced by the state. The Bible says no. The mission of manhood is bound up with fathering."[3]

The Apostle Paul (when writing to his mentee Timothy) spoke of a future time:

"People will be lovers of themselves, lovers of money, boastful, proud, abusive, disobedient to their parents..." (2 Timothy 3:2).

In a socialist society, the goal is for the state to take over the role of protector, provider, and teacher. Loyalty can then lead to children rebelling from their parental authority to serve the state. The state ultimately rejects all authority, even that of God .

Certainly, the Bible calls for obedience to ruling authorities (except where the state violates the principles of God). Jesus said, *"Give to Caesar what is Caesar's, and to God what is God's"* (Matthew 22: 21b).

However, there is a Biblical warning to be watchful. There is an enemy out to devour the foundation of the family, which God establishes:

"Be alert and of sober mind. Your enemy the devil prowls around like a roaring lion looking for someone to devour" (1 Peter 5:8).

Fathers, mothers, and children NOT grounded in biblical truth can eventually fall prey to an enemy that doesn't just want their allegiance, but their souls.

HERE ARE OTHER WAYS THE FAMILY IS CURRENTLY LOSING ITS STRENGTH:

1. *Time constraints* (prioritizing activities over preserving connection)

2. *Declining focus on spirituality* (making the secular world more available)

3. *An obsession with social media* (leading to a lack of social skills and isolation)

4. *Educational failures* (reconstructing history vs. historical reality)

5. *Identity and gender confusion* (based on feelings)

6. *Deconstruction of faith* (undoing what is true for what is wanted)

7. *Father absence* (detrimental to all the above)

"According to the Census Bureau's statistics on families, approximately 18.4 million children now live without a father in the home. That's one in four children in the country-double the number since 1960."[4]

Additionally, socialism no longer sees the Heavenly Father as the ultimate authority. The Bible (God's Word spoken to you) is replaced with relativism. When this happens, freedom to do whatever one wants is lived out at the cost of law and order. Individual needs also trump those of others.

When an individual defines what is good and what is bad, this leads to the demise of society. All of today's new definitions begin to crash into one another. What is left are no absolutes, no moral code, and no ten commandments. The outcome is societal decay and disorder.

The Heavenly Father helps lay the tracks on which a child will take his/her journey in life. He demonstrates and teaches principles which are timeless, cultureless, and non-negotiable.

Earthly fathers who model their lives after THE FATHER help to establish children that are selfless, secure, and set on doing what is right.

In Proverbs 22:6, King Solomon (who was full of wisdom) said, "Train a child in the way he should go, and when he is old he will not turn from it."

Be mindful and prayerful today for your children. If you do not lead them, someone else will.

The 1974 top-100 folk rock song *"Cat's in The Cradle"* by Harry Chapin had a lasting impact on me. Yet, like many songs with a catchy jingle, it tells a sad tale.

It's narrated by a man who becomes a father. Not long after his son's birth, the father is repeatedly unable to spend time with him due to his job's demands, despite his son's desire for his time and attention. The tragedy is that the son grows up to be an absent father. I encourage you to listen to the song if you are not familiar with it.

This is a cycle that needs to be broken, or it will repeat through the generations. Make the choice to be a present father.

DISCUSSION QUESTIONS

1. What was your family like growing up?

2. Did you do things together? What are some special memories?

3. I wish my family would have_____ _____.

4. What positive characteristics have you carried into your family?

5. What are some negative carryovers?

6. What societal distractions concern you for your children?

NOTES

CHAPTER 3:

Father as Mentor

In the face of a fracturing society, we need fathers to be mentors. Where an earthly Father is deficient or is fully absent, an additional man can model and instill wisdom, character, and love where it is needed. Better yet, if this man is a follower of God, he will ultimately encourage another to seek the ultimate Father.

In my decades of ministry, I truly believe the most effective use of my time and energy has been investing in others. It's also a two-way street. As others have learned from me, I have learned from them. One of my greatest joys is seeing those that I have mentored become far more effective in serving than I ever could.

One surprise I received while writing this book was a contribution from Mike Stout. I was Mike's pastor during his teenage years and have mentored throughout his adult years in Christian ministry. Honestly, I have never considered myself as an influencer. However, what he shares about our mentoring relationship proves that God

49

can use anyone who is open to share his or her life with another.

Immediately, two words spring to mind that have characterized Rick's mentoring relationship with me over the years. The first word is *understanding*. This goes beyond understanding my viewpoint and what I mean. Instead, it encapsulates the idea of completely identifying with my situation, my thought process, my challenges, and my emotions. I vividly remember a time in my life as a young husband, young father, and young youth pastor in ministry. My church situation at the time was full of rocky roads. Challenges and internal power struggles within the church leadership splintered out of control, and, as the underling on staff, I became the whipping boy for the pastor and for the eldership through manipulation and church politics. In my inexperienced and idealistic mind, I wanted to believe the best about everyone, and I wrestled with the words and behaviors that blasted me. I would much more willingly accept that, somehow, I was inadequate and had failed than to believe that what I experienced from others was so hurtful and unprovoked. I reached out to Rick and confided in him about my situation. I was careful to be honest and transparent while trying to avoid speaking poorly of anyone else. I tried to own as much of the blame as I possibly could. However, as I shared the facts, Rick blurted out in astonishment, *"How could they do that? That's not even Christlike!"* In a moment, he gave me permission—without bitterness or anger—to admit and recognize that some people in the situation were being hurtful and ungodly toward me. It gave me freedom just to have someone acknowledge that. It validated my hurt but did not give me permission to hold on to it. One Rickism that has always stuck with me and has been repeated within my family in ministry time and time again is this: *"You have to have the skin of a rhinoceros and the heart of a dove."* Acknowledge the hurt. Do not let it cling to you. Respond in love.

Secondly, Rick always speaks *affirmation* into my life. Years later, as I started in a new ministry as a chaplain, Rick continued to pour positivity into me. He would often say, *"You are very insightful in that observation. You are exactly right. Not everyone can pick up on that."* Rick consistently saw strength in me and would suggest and imply that I had leadership potential and discernment that could be used in greater ways in ministry. Initially, I doubted that potential, but Rick's consistent affirmations and calling out leadership gifts within me began to shape me over time. Sometimes he guides me and offers perspective, but usually he affirms what he already sees in me. His gift to me in this way has transformed my personal ministry to others. His words resonate within my mind and heart as I talk with others, and I find myself looking for ways to call out greatness and giftedness in them—simply to identify it and let them hear that greatness is seen in them. My son made me a display a couple of years ago with a proverb that he made up himself. It sits on my desk and simply reads, *"He who builds others up will have a strong foundation."* This is a testimony to the desire to call others out to greatness that my son sees in me, and it is a gift that over the years has been mentored into me through Rick's example. Always turning the spotlight to someone else's strengths, Rick has frequently said to me, "*I want my ceiling to be your floor.*"

BIBLICAL MENTORSHIP

In the Old Testament, Moses mentored Joshua to prepare him for future leadership of the nation of Israel. Moses was an imperfect man, as all men are. Yet, as a servant of God, Moses played a vital role in listening to God's instruction so that the entire nation of Israel was freed from their Egyptian captivity.

Joshua followed closely beside Moses for forty years on their journey to the Promised Land (modern day Israel). He would have witnessed him ascending to Mount Sinai to receive God's law - a defining moment in his closeness with God and his leadership of the nation. He also would have seen him strike the rock (when the people demanded water) without asking for God's help - a consequential moment in Moses' life that ultimately ended it. Through it all, Moses kept Joshua close, showing him *how* to lead, *how not* to lead, and *who* to follow.

Paul, an apostle of Jesus, is an all-star in the Bible (despite being a murderer of Christians when he was called Saul). He is a primary author of many books in the New

Testament, as well as a martyr for his faith. However, without Barnabas, a mentor in his life, Paul most likely would not have reached such heights. Acts 9:27 says, "But Barnabas took him and brought him to the apostles." Barnabas believed in Paul and his impact was great.

In fatherhood, a good father mentors his children, hoping they will do the same for others. "Be a mentor to your children as well as to other young adults. Offer them leadership, but don't treat them as children. Foster their growth and independence."[5]

MENTORING MOMENTS

There was a time mentoring was the primary way people acquired their profession. A mentee learned by coming alongside one who was skilled at the trade. The less-skilled apprentice then received hands-on experience, while the skilled teacher passed on his trade, gaining a co-worker.

Today, we tend to educate almost exclusively in the classroom setting. We choose to convey book knowledge without providing as much hands-on experience. Public education is the primary voice shaping the minds and morals of our children.

In the past, the daily teachings of the extended family were instrumental in shaping the lives of their children. They were the most influential mentors teaching the trades that were to be passed down from generation to generation.

This isn't an opinion of old ways versus modern ways, but of the structure all mankind was intended to learn from since the beginning of time. In the Bible, virtually all instruction took place in a mentoring setting. The Jewish prayer (called *the Shema*) found in (Deuteronomy 6:4-9: says:

Hear, O Israel: The Lord our God, the Lord is one. Love the Lord your God with all our heart and with all your soul and with all your strength. These commandments that I give you today are to be upon our hearts. Impress them on our children. Talk about them when you sit at home and when you walk along the road, when you lie down and when you get up. Tie them as symbols on our hands and bind them on your foreheads. Write them on the door frames of your house and on your gates.

Since all mankind came from one man, Adam, and one woman, Eve, we are all connected to the same mentoring story. Jethro taught Moses, Moses taught Joshua. Naomi taught Ruth, Elijah taught Elisha. Elizabeth taught Mary. Jesus taught His disciples. Barnabas taught Paul. Paul taught Timothy. Priscilla and Aquila taught Apollos, and the list goes on.

Sadly, today fewer leaders are finishing well; they aren't living as a good example. There is a growing void of leaders positively helping to develop our society. I am convinced that a contributing factor to the lack of leaders is a lack of mentoring. Mentoring is a special relationship between two people where they share life experiences. Part of those experiences entail both successes and failures.

Everyone needs accountability, encouragement, and shared experiences to grow in a positive way. People who have had an impact on society rarely reach their goals alone. I have always felt successful people stand on the shoulders of a network of mentoring relationships that they have had in life.

Although the Bible provides examples of mentorship, some believe the term "*mentor*" first appeared in Greek mythology in Homer's *The Odyssey*. In this epic story, Ulysses asked a wise man named *Mentor* to care for his son, Telemachus, while he was fighting in the Trojan War. Mentor not only taught the boy in book learning, but also in practical daily living. Telemachus grew up to help his father recover his kingdom.

Recently, I was encouraged to listen to a missionary who had served for many years in China. This individual had been in denominational leadership, but shared that he was turning his attention away from administration to mentoring Chinese pastors. His mission with the people is clear; he wants his influence to last, so he is leaving his imprint on others.

In many cultures, vulnerability is seen as a weakness. Yet, a major part of mentoring is being real in sharing struggles. Mentors are people who care about other people.

In the tyranny of the urgent, they invest time in building relationships and meeting that person at their point of need. "A mentor is not a person who can do the work better than his followers; he is a person who can get his followers to do the work better than he can." [6]

Mentoring is a sharing of life experiences, one to the other. As 1 Thessalonians 2:8b says, *"...we loved you so much that we were delighted to share with you not only the gospel of God but our lives as well."*

Mentoring is what we leave in others that lives on after we are gone. Truly, success is evidenced in succession. Who are you currently investing yourself in?

ESSENTIALS IN MENTORING

1. Mentor in a holistic manner.

    Don't just focus on your personal passions. Consider the other person as a whole. As James 1:19 says, "My dear brothers and sisters, take note of this: Everyone should be quick to listen, slow to speak and slow to become angry."

    Do your best to be faithful to the time you are given. This relationship will take patience.

2. Ask questions so your mentee can focus on developing a better spiritual life.

Questions such as, *"What does your prayer life look like?"* or *"How do you apply scriptures in your life?"*

3. Live (a righteous) life before your mentee that is worthy of being followed.

    In Matthew 4:19, Jesus says: *"Come follow me, Jesus said, and I will send you out to fish for people."*

4. Pray for and with your mentee.

    Prayer is an acknowledgement of a needed relationship with God. It's a reminder to your mentee that you are as imperfect as they are, but that He is the ultimate help in every situation.

5. Let your mentee know you are available.

    When you set a time, show up! This alone will make you credible to their care. When you meet, keep the time concise. Stay in contact regularly, but allow for a healthy space, so they can also be reminded to depend on God.

6. Recognize that different mentees require different learning styles.

    Take your time in getting to know your mentee. In mentoring (either father/son or man/man), pray for a relational bonding. The goal is to share mutual knowledge and life experiences that better both sides.

MODELING MANHOOD

What is a man? The Biblical answer (seen in Genesis 1:27), is that he is made in God's *"own image."*

However, today's culture considers traditional manhood as a shifting character. Being masculine at all is often considered dated and defective. Just look at men's roles in movies today (in contrast to a decade ago) and you will see a stark difference. Men are struggling with what true manhood should be.

Traditional manhood stands out in opposition to gender-neutral thinking. The strength a good man shows in the life of a son should be not seen as a weakness.

Absent fathers are also leading to further the problem. Young boys seek male examples to follow. When there are fewer *exemplary* men to follow, *bad examples* become cheap stand-ins. This can create disconnected, misguided, and undisciplined sons.

It's no wonder that some look to find acceptance within wrong groups, such as gangs, providing them with a false-protective family structure.

Let's take a look at Biblical manhood.

JOSHUA WAS A MODEL

Joshua was mentored by Moses. He was instructed by Moses in Biblical truths which are timeless, cultureless, and non-negotiable. In the face of societal and leadership challenges, the Heavenly Father spoke to him these words: *"...Be strong and courageous. Do not be terrified; do not be discouraged, for the Lord your God will be with you wherever you go"* (Joshua 1:9).

Notice Joshua's declaration before those he led: *"But if serving the Lord seems undesirable to you, then choose for yourselves this day whom you will serve, whether the gods your forefathers served beyond the river, or the gods of the Amorite, in whose land you are living. But as for me and my household, we will serve the Lord"* (Joshua 24:15).

Does that last line sound familiar? Joshua's leadership was so influential that households today aim to "serve the Lord" as he did (often putting that exact verse on the wall).

ABRAHAM WAS A MODEL

In providing these *models of manhood*, I am not saying that these biblical leaders/fathers were perfect. Earthly fathers are a work in progress. However, they do provide us with examples we can examine in our pilgrimage to be better men in the roles of father and husband.

Fathers need to be examples of men of faith. *Abraham was a genuine man of faith.* A favorite verse of mine is found in Genesis 15:5, *"Abram believed the Lord, and he credited it to him as righteousness."*

Abram, before he was renamed Abraham by the Lord, obeyed the Lord's leading. He left his country and his people without a clear map as to where he was going. He simply went, and by going modeled genuine faith:

In Genesis 12:1 we read, *"The Lord said to Abram , 'Leave your country, your people and your father's household and go to the land I will show you.'"*

What faith! Even when we go on a short vacation, we usually have an itinerary. We plan places to stay and make reservations. We map out great places where we want to eat. We even set a time to arrive back to the safety and security of home.

God asked Abram to leave his country. This was not a one-week trip to Florida. He was leaving his father's household without knowing his final destination.

Are you kidding me?! Can you imagine the reaction he got from his countrymen and his father's household? They thought he had lost his mind! What about his immediate family and servants? *(I have a suspicion Abram's wife Sarai was probably not a happy camper.)*

I remember (in the pastorate) when the Lord would call

me to a new church. When led, I could accept a call and relocate my family within several weeks. This was never easy. However, Malissa would often say:

"The Lord speaks to you, not to me. Just tell me when to pack."

God did not provide Abram with an itinerary. He simply said, *"I will show you."* Yet, He didn't send Abram out wondering what was to come. God made Abram promises if he would trust Him. God declared He would:

1. show him the way

2. bless him

3. make his name great

4. bless those who blessed Abram

5. curse those who were trouble for Abram

6. bless all the people of the earth through Abram

After these pronouncements from the Almighty, you would think (from a human perspective) that Abram would have begun with the *"What if...?"* questions. *Yet, he didn't.* Abram had faith in a Heavenly Father:

In Genesis 14:1a it says, *"So Abram left, as the Lord had told him..."*

This act of following God reminds me of what an Italian-French poet expressed in what I call the God nudge, in helping one take the step of faith.

"Come to the edge," he said.

They said, "We are afraid."

"Come to the edge," he said.

They came.

He pushed them...and they flew.

Guillaume Apollinaire

LESS THAN MODEL FATHERS

Let us not forget there is only one perfect Father, our Heavenly Father.

We have looked at the lives of two model fathers in the Bible. Now we will shift our attention to two less than stellar fathers in the Old Testament. (As a comfort, the Bible is filled with flawed men made better when they modeled their lives after God.)

ELI THE PRIEST

Eli was a Jewish priest living in the times of the judges and who served God at Shiloh. He is known for his conversation with Hannah as she prayed for a child who grew to be Samuel the prophet.

As a priest, Eli was a mediator between God and man (a

counselor/teacher). However, his faithfulness to God was not modeled to his sons Hophni and Phineas. In 1 Samuel 2:12, Samuel literally described these sons as wicked:

"They showed contempt for the Lord's offering, they slept around with women who were servants at the entrance to the Tent of Meetings."

Where was Eli when his sons were behaving this way? It would seem Eli spent more time at his priestly duties when the boys were young and failed to direct them in the ways of the Lord. Finally, at an old age, Eli questions them:

"Why do you do such things? I hear from all the people about these wicked deeds of yours" (I Samuel 2:23). Would Eli have addressed these issues without the Israelites pointing out his sons' sins? No surprise, his sons did not listen to their father. They had no foundational faith. Therefore, they did as they pleased, not fearing God or the consequences of their lifestyles.

The Apostle Paul wrote:

> *"Children, obey your parents in the Lord, for this is right. Honor your father and mother which is the first commandment with a promise- that it may go well with you and that you may enjoy a long life on the earth"* *(Ephesians 6:1-4).*

The consequence of Eli's failed role as a father, teacher, and disciplinarian ultimately led to the death of his sons. When exposed, I believe Eli thought more of his sons' behavior (and how this reflected on him) than how the Heavenly Father should have been modeled all along in his sons' lives. Sadly in I Samuel 2:29 it says, *"A curse fell on his lineage"* because he failed to restrain them.

Despite Samuel himself capturing these warnings, 1 Samuel 8:3 says of his own two sons, Joel and Abijah, *"But his sons did not follow his ways. They turned aside after dishonest gain and accepted bribes and perverted justice."* Both Eli and Samuel did not do well in parenting.

Children are a blessing from Father God. With this gift comes the privilege and responsibility of introducing them to their Heavenly Father. This is made clear in Deuteronomy 6:6-7, "These commandments that I give you today are to be on your hearts. Impress them on your children. Talk about them when you sit at home and when you walk along the road, when you lie down and when you get up."

It is not only by teaching them words, but it is also living a lifestyle before them that is reflective of the image of God. When these tracks are laid, it is less likely that they will depart from the path laid before them as they grow. This in no way denies their free will, but certainly increases the odds they will go God's way if they are instructed in *the* way.

SAUL THE KING

Israel wanted to have a king like other nations. This spoke volumes about their lack of dependance on the person of God. They wanted a king they could see, a figurehead they could follow. They wanted to be like the world.

1 Samuel 8:6b says the people demanded of Samuel, a prophet of God, *"Give us a king to lead us."* In this, they were rejecting God as sovereign. God granted Israel their request for a king, but as Scripture tells us, there are always consequences to demanding human will over God's will. God even tried to warn them:

> *"Now listen to them; but warn them solemnly and let them know what the king who will reign over them will claim as his rights" (1 Samuel 8:9).*

God then prompted Samuel to tell the people what would happen if they got their way, explaining in detail what this king *"will take"* from them, their sons, and their daughters. But the people refused to listen. They wanted a king at any cost.

Thus, Samuel was directed by God to pick Saul as the first king of Israel. Physically, Saul was attractive; he was a head taller than most. Saul even had a good start as king by leading Israel in a successful campaign against the Ammonites.

Unfortunately, Saul failed in fully obeying God. Where God sought a man after His own heart, Saul became more focused on placating people than pleasing God:

> *"Then Saul said to Samuel, 'I have sinned. I violated the Lord's command and your instruction. I was afraid of the people and so I gave in to them" (I Samuel 15:14).*

It was a devastating time for the people of Israel when the Spirit of the Lord departed from Saul. As Saul struggled to hold power, an evil spirit from God tormented him. Nations began to rise up against the Israelites. During his forty-two year reign, it was obvious Saul was only a small king before the sovereign King.

JONATHAN AND DAVID

Interestingly, one very special friendship surfaced in the midst of Saul's sin. This was the deep bond between Saul's son Jonathan and his friend David: *"Jonathan became one in spirit with David, and he loved him as himself"* (I Samuel 8:1b).

Even Saul knew Jonathan was on David's side. On two separate occasions Saul threw a spear at them - first at David and another time at his son Jonathan (after he came to David's defense). Saul was so incensed that he cared only for protecting himself.

66

Tragically, both Saul and his sons, including Jonathan, died in battle against the Philistines. Ironically, David himself would be the one to take the throne. Yet, even after Jonathan's death, David appeared to carry a special place in his heart for Jonathan, evidenced in his caring and provision for Mephibosheth (the disabled son of Jonathan). God would continue to care for the Israelites by David's bloodline, not Saul's, which eventually led to Jesus.

There is a ray of hope in this story, even for us, of a failed father and king. Even if a father fails, his children can choose a different path. Inheriting the family business is not the chief aim of life, nor will it necessarily bring happiness.

We have to choose not to give in to the fear of failure, or succumbing to the grip of jealousy. The right path might not lead to what the world defines as success.

God places people in our lives to show us they have a heart after God. People don't love us because of our power or positions in life, but love us for who we are. Such people are people who we can trust. Such was the bond between Jonathan and David.

FAIR WEATHER FRIENDS

I have discovered, over seven decades of life, that fair weather friends come and go. Such friends are present in good times, but not in times of trouble. They go from our lives as quickly as they have come, like the wind, leaving little trace of permanence.

I taught my daughters in their teen years not to compromise their values for seeming friendships. I taught them, *"Those around you now will largely be absent from your life in the future."*

Most people have a number of acquaintances, but have few true friends. Close friendships have been in decline in recent years due societal pressures leading to greater polarization and loneliness. As I heard someone say once, *"People don't discuss issues anymore; it's my way or the highway."*

Loneliness is a growing issue in society. Fathers as well as men in general have difficulty in finding deep friendships like that of David and Jonathan. A single dad can feel isolated in finding connections to voice his need for help in parenting. Women feel more comfortable in reaching out for support from others. However, most men can't even define what a close friend is. Instead, they equate acquaintances as friends.

In Proverbs 17:17, Solomon says in regard to friendship:

> *"A friend loves at all times, and a brother is born for adversity."*

EVIDENCE OF TRUE FRIENDSHIP

- Friends love each other no matter what.

- Friends respect each other.

- Friends speak the truth.

- Friends trust.

- Friends are fun to be with.

- Friends affirm one another.

- To have a friend, you must be a friend.

DISCUSSION QUESTIONS:

1. Can you think of another model of a Biblical father?

2. Why is modeling manhood a challenge to secular thinking?

3. Did you have a mentor?

4. What are some ways a dad can mentor his children?

5. Why did Eli fail as a father?

NOTES:

CHAPTER 4:

Father/Dad

Is there a difference between being a father and being a dad? Absolutely! A father can just be a biological contributor.

A growing number of children today are living without a father present. With a growing focus on individualism, the traditional family is suffering.

Granted, anyone can be a father. However, only those who take up the mantle of love and responsibility can earn the title of "Dad."

What a Present Dad Does:

(Check off the ones in this list that resonate with your dad):

☐ He spends time with his children.

☐ He provides.

☐ He listens.

☐ He speaks lovingly.

☐ His touch is meaningful (hugs).

☐ He's caring.

☐ He's honest.

☐ He demonstrates loving actions.

☐ He shows emotions and vulnerability.

☐ He demonstrates dependency on His Heavenly Father.

☐ He encourages those around him.

☐ He's available (even when he is busy).

☐ He's a teacher/mentor.

☐ He's a good example of manhood.

☐ He provides security.

CAN YOU LIST FIVE ADDITIONAL CHARACTERISTICS OF A GOOD DAD?

1.

2.

3.

4.

5.

THE ABSENT FATHER

These are some contributing factors to fatherlessness:

1. Divorce

2. Separation

3. Death

4. Incarceration

5. Poverty

6. Greater dropout rates in schools

7. Drug and alcohol

8. Mental health issues

9. Running away from home

10. Teen pregnancy

Currently, as I am writing this book, many are coming to the conclusion that fatherlessness is a major contributor to the deterioration of our society. One thing both conservatives and liberals can agree on is fatherlessness is one of the greater problems we are facing as a nation.

Today, children born out of wedlock have reached forty percent. Some estimate that up to thirty percent of children are cared for by single parents. This is alarming. As C.S. Lewis wrote, *"Fatherhood must be at the core of the universe."*[7]

My seminary professor at Asbury Theological Seminary, Don Joy, claims that:

"Men with a damaged father connection will be healed only to the extent that they can describe the loss and pain."[8]

Back to our initial question. *Is there a difference between being a father and being a dad?* We have learned that any man can father a child, but to be a dad, well, that is another story.

BEING A DAD IS A CHOICE

There was a time when some misguided souls would preach this familiar phrase:

"Children should be seen and not heard."

However, one major choice in fatherhood is to be present - not only physically, but also emotionally. There is a power in presence, but being near someone doesn't communicate the act of actually entering in to someone's life. It is a choice to be a present listener, responder, and uplifter.

When I served as a pastor, I always felt it was a special occasion when a child would approach me to ask a question or just share what was on his/her mind. In the midst of those moments, sometimes an adult would attempt to come by and interrupt. *(In other words, they thought what they had to say was more important than me listening to a child.)*

I would respectfully tell the adult that I would be with them after my conversation with the child was done. I instructed my staff that children always had access to me. It's important to note that Jesus held the same view, even while busy with adults in His ministry:

> *"Let the little children come to me, and do not hinder them, for the kingdom of heaven belongs to such as these" (Matthew 19:14).*

Dads must be emotionally present for their children. Some children are living in an angry environment. Men often determine for themselves that their anger is acceptable because it results in the silence of others. However, anger is never a safe emotion, and many fathers are simply repeating the anger environment they grew up in. This generational curse of anger needs to be broken.

Any level of anger can be modeled down to children. For example, men can act like a hungry bear when they are hungry. *(I always advise wives to feed the "hungry bear" before they get into any in-depth conversation.)* However, even this type of anger isn't excusable.

I recall driving home from a long day in the office. I didn't want to drag the dynamic of the day into the home and take out my frustrations on my wife and the kids.

Before I entered our house, I stopped to address what I called my "burden bush" right outside of our front door. I would say to the bush (and to myself), "*I am going to leave my burdens of the day in the bush. If issues need to be picked up, I will pick them up here when I leave in the morning.*"

This simple act helped me stop and remind myself that I was entering into a special place; a place where my wife and children lived with *me*. I did not want to dump my issues that they could not fix on them.

Dad, hear this warning:

If your emotional tank is empty, you have the potential to strike out in anger against those you love.

You might wonder:

How do I replenish my tank when I am stressed out?

What about when I feel like I have few reserves?

You need to find balance in life. This is not easy, and it takes constant discipline. As I often told my girls (when we would have what I liked to call "car clinic" together), *"Take care of your car, and your car will take care of you."*

The same discipline applies here. Give yourself check-ups regularly. Stop in your tracks when you are steering yourself and others in the wrong direction. Take care of yourself and do not excuse the warning lights of your negative emotions. Ask God and others for help. Otherwise, you run the potential of wearing yourself and those you love out.

Life balance is one of the greatest challenges today. Work can demand a big chunk of our energy, and most work environments are not sensitive to our need to find time for family and friends.

In my roles as pastor/chaplain, I've never heard a man on his deathbed say to me, *"I wish I had spent more time at work."* Yet, some men spend their entire careers ascending the ladder of success to find when they get to the top, they have put their ladder on the wrong building. When a man neglects his home, his home suffers.

WHAT IF YOUR EARTHLY FATHER HAS PASSED?

Even if your dad has passed on, you can still be plagued with inner questions. You may wonder:

1. Dad, why didn't you tell me you loved me?

2. Why didn't you tell me about your family?

3. Why didn't you ever hug me?

4. What caused you to be an angry person?

5. Did you love Mom?

THE EMPTY CHAIR EXERCISE

When I served as a family and marital counselor in High Point, North Carolina, I would on occasion ask a person with a father issue to talk to an empty chair in my office. I would ask them to imagine their father was sitting in that chair. Nothing was off limits, and sometimes they would erupt emotionally, and begin to express the depths of their hurt. This was sometimes a gateway into their freedom to open up, and would often begin the healing process.

I don't know where I first heard the following statement, but it makes a lot of sense:

"I started talking to myself. Then I started listening to myself. Then I had to quit listening to myself, because I was giving myself bad advice."

Seek out Godly counsel. It could be a pastor, chaplain, or counselor who will be the key to helping you unlock the door to emotional and spiritual healing.

DISCUSSION QUESTIONS:

1. How did you refer to the first man in your life? (*Did you call him Father, Dad, his first name, etc.?*)

2. Did you feel your dad was present in your life?

3. If your dad has passed, what do you miss most about him?

4. If your father was absent, what consequences have you experienced?

5. What was out of balance in your dad's life?

NOTES:

_____

_____

_____

_____

_____

_____

_____

_____

_____

_____

_____

_____

_____

_____

_____

_____

_____

_____

_____

_____

CHAPTER 5:

Finding Balance

In our quest to find balance in the workaday world, men and women find themselves on the precipice of burnout. Too much tuning into the W-O-R-L-D will leave one longing for a sabbath, as the W-O-R-D of God models from the beginning. "All of us, I'm afraid, are out of balance and suffering for it. We succeed, but experience only a momentary sense of success before the old emptiness returns."[9]

In the very first book of the Bible, after God created the world in a span of six days, He rested on the seventh day (Genesis 2:2-3). He didn't stop because He was subject to fatigue. He could have chosen to create constantly, forever, without exhaustion. Yet, by choosing to model rest one day of the week He provides an example for man to learn from.

BELOW ARE FOUR AREAS WHERE YOU MAY BE STRUGGLING TO FIND BALANCE IN YOUR LIFE:

1.Recognition.

God appointed Adam to care for the Garden of Eden. Managing the garden was his job, where he found recognition and identity. While there, Adam even named every animal.

Yet, there is a declaration in the Ten Commandments calling for a sabbath rest on the seventh day (Deuteronomy). Like a stop light, there is an intended pause from the normal works of one's hands.

In Japan, they actually have a word for work that leads one to job-related exhaustion and death. The word is "karoshi." Can you imagine an epitaph that reads: *"DIED AT HIS DESK."*

Men can be too centered on work, drawing the majority of their self-worth from their labor. As an employee, men forget they can easily be replaced. Think about it. When two men meet for the first time, one of the first questions often asked is, *"What do you do for a living?"* When women meet, they are more likely to pull out a picture of their kids and grandkids. It is far better to build relationships than to build a career. This is how one best leaves a legacy in others.

2. Relaxation.

At 75 years of age, I need more rest. I jokingly say, *"Every time I get still, I go to sleep."* Sleep is not optional; it is a necessity to health and happiness.

More people than ever are struggling to get a good night's sleep. (*If you don't believe me, just count the number of sleep aid commercials advertised these days.*)

How much sleep do you need? *Well,* that depends on *you.* If you aren't rested when you wake up in the morning, maybe it's time to go to bed earlier. Eating late, bringing work home, and neglecting exercise are a few contributors to a lack of proper rest.

Also, it's not good to get into in-depth conversations late at night. If at all possible, try to avoid discussing heavy issues before bed. This often leads to arguments (as emotional reserves are low).

3. Recreation.

We need to have fun in our lives!

My dad was a good golfer. When he wasn't working, he enjoyed playing a round of golf. He even sported the stereotypical golf hat while he played. However, golf wasn't for me. It wasn't fun; it was work!

TIP: If what you enjoy feels more like work (or extra competition), you need to find something else to do that's fun. You should feel better after enjoying recreation than when you started.

Don't feel guilty taking time for yourself. You will find there will be more of you to give afterwards.

Also, stick with what works for you. When people would try to get me to join a gym, they would go through an extensive list of what they had to offer. They would then ask me:

"What do you like to do?"

"Run!" was my response.

I didn't need to join a gym to run (and actually prefer to be outside), so for me, I could skip the gym and enjoy what I enjoy for free. (These days it's walking in the park with my wife Malissa.)

Find the right outlet for you. Don't get into the mentality that you must win at any cost. If you must compete in something to blow off steam, learn to be a gracious loser. If you make it too intense, it will continue to take from you.

Also, it would be great to schedule fun events with your family. One vacation a year is not what I am talking about. Find a regular family rhythm that is fun. Give everyone a time together with you to look forward to. Friday night "family night" was a regular event when my girls were growing up. It was a break from our norm when we could go out to eat, go home and watch a movie/play a board game, or do something together we didn't do the rest of the week.

As a corporate chaplain, I would ask employees, *"What are you looking forward to?"* The vast majority had nothing come to mind except getting off work on time. This isn't healthy. We need *"Calgon, take me away"* moments - naps, trips to a favorite store, even taking time to remember a great memory from the past. It doesn't have to be complicated. Stopping for your favorite cup of coffee (as I like to do) can bring simple fun.

Too many of us try to package our emotional release within a week's vacation. Yet, we leave no room for rest when the itinerary is so structured.

I love Jesus' words here:

> *"Come to me, all you who are weary and burdened, and I will give you rest. Take my yoke upon you and learn from me, for I am gentle and humble in heart, and you will find rest for your souls. For my yoke is easy and my burden is light"* (Matthew 11:28-28).

4. Reflection.

We have talked about the importance of physical rest. However, there is another form of rest that is key, that being spiritual rest.

Physical rest can only take you so far. We also need soul rest. Can you say to yourself right now, *"It is well with my soul?"*

Once, I was planning to speak at a business seminar. I had my assigned topic and was considering what I should say to the group. Then, I felt this inner stirring to forgo my assigned topic and instead ask the group a question. I began to debate within myself (*Shouldn't I just do what they told me to do?*). However, I have learned to listen to the inner voice of the Holy Spirit and knew what I needed to do.

After my introduction, I stood behind the podium to give the predetermined address. I put my notes aside and simply looked at the audience and said:

"Is it well with your soul?"

A hush fell over the room. I looked to the back of the room and noticed a lady was crying. Amazed, the CEO leaned over and whispered to the man beside him: *"This is of God."*

It was one of those moments of divine presence, which to this day brings me deep personal reflection.

I had a second occurrence of divine prompting while I attended Nyack College in Nyack, New York from 1969-72. There, I was president of the Missions Committee, which was responsible for planning a weekly chapel service. Our own college students and those from Jaffery School of Missions regularly attended.

Prior to one chapel meeting, I'd read Robert Coleman's

book *One Divine Moment*, relating to revival that had taken place at Asbury College in Wilmore, Kentucky. [10] The night before the chapel service, we prayed as a committee, and I shared with them that I felt that God wanted to give us a divine moment in the chapel the next day (we had a noted speaker scheduled from out of state).

Before anything else was said, I stood up before the gathering of students and faculty, paused, and said:

"I believe God wants to do something..."

Again, I paused, this time, saying nothing.

Then, a divine presence *fell* on that place. Students started moving forward to kneel and pray. The special speaker never got to speak that day. Class attendance was optional that day as many remained in the chapel to seek a divine moment.   True soul rest and revival came to the college campus in October of 1971.

Man needs soul rest. I believe we are made up of body, soul, and spirit. Just as the physical body needs renewal, so does the soul. The soul, without getting too theological, is the eternal part of a person. It's what lives on when the body dies.

We have seen in Genesis that God rested on the seventh day after His work of creation. The fourth commandment says:

Remember the Sabbath day by keeping it

holy. Six days you shall labor and do all your work. But the seventh day is a Sabbath to the Lord our God. On it you shall not do any work, neither you, nor your son or daughter, nor your servant or maid servant, nor your animal, nor the alien with your gates. For in six days the Lord made heaven and the earth, the seas, and all that is in the, but he rested on the seventh day. Therefore, the Lord blessed the Sabbath day and made it holy.

Exodus 20:8-11

We need a sabbath rest at least once a week. It is a time to renew our souls by reflecting on God our Heavenly Father. This renews the forever part of us. The soul is eternal, but needs time for regular refreshing.

One of the greatest forms of renewal is through worship. I define worship as acknowledging the worth of God. Worship is not restricted to one day of the week in a church building. Yet, I look forward to going to church on Sunday and joining in with fellow believers in singing, sharing, praying and being instructed in Biblical truth. When together in Christian community, there is a corporate expression of reverence, love, trust in God the Father, God the Son, and God the Holy Spirit.

I currently live on a bluff overlooking Shoal Creek in Florence, Alabama. I have grown more to worship God through the beauty of His creation in this setting. The rising of the sun and the setting of the sun is a reflection of divine order and beauty. Every time a bald eagle passes overhead, I am called to worship. Every time I see a doe with her fawn, I declare His creation is marvelous.

Ask God to direct you to find balance in everything, including your soul. This will better allow you to live a life of *THANKSLIVING*.

DISCUSSION QUESTIONS:

1. How do you struggle with life balance?

2. Why do men draw so much of their identity from work?

3. What areas do you need to work on (recognition/ relaxation/ recreation/ reflection)?

4. Have you ever experienced soul rest? If so, how?

5. Do you have a sabbath rest/worship day?

NOTES:

_____

_____

_____

_____

_____

_____

_____

_____

_____

_____

_____

_____

_____

_____

_____

_____

_____

_____

CHAPTER 6:

Finding a Father Figure

What if your father is absent in your life? Would it be beneficial for you to have a stand-in?

Though you are not given the opportunity to choose your biological father, it is possible to allow another earthly man who is willing to adopt you as his own access to your life.

However, a fill-in father should fit seamlessly into your life. The want of this relationship can't be forced with just anyone. A proper fit may take time to discover and develop.

A stand-in father cannot take away the pain that your absent father has added to your life. Yet, when someone naturally offers up his presence, care, and availability in your life, it doesn't hurt to allow yourself the opportunity for experiences with another dad-like figure. Better yet, if the stand-in father reflects his Heavenly Father, you can be assured you will never be without the security of an available father again.

When I was pastoring in Port Charlotte, Florida, and Missy was in high school, her best friend, Laura Sherwood (Way), began coming over to our house. Like Missy, she was the oldest of her siblings. However, unlike Missy, her dad was not in the picture or in her home. Yet, in our house of three girls she fit in like a fourth sister.

When Laura later became engaged, she asked *me* to walk her down the aisle and officiate her wedding. She chose me as her stand-in dad. On one of the most important days of her life, she gave me one of the greatest privileges one may have. Today, though separated by miles, we still touch base by phone on holidays and special occasions.

Here is what Laura shares in regard to her ultimate adoption:

"Rick was a *consistent* father figure, a great one, in my life." An earthy father relates to or foreshadows the Heavenly Father.

The difference is, because our earthly father is not perfect (and passes away), our Heavenly Father is *constant*. Consistency is awesome with our earthly father, but our Heavenly Father is the only one who can be *constant*.

Who is a candidate for an adoptive Dad?

As with Laura, it could be a dad in the family of a friend.

94

There the child can experience the dynamics of a healthy nuclear family. The child can experience conversations at their dinner table, observe their daily interactions with one another, and learn how to model loving relationships. Having an open door to walk through with a warm and welcoming invitation on the other side is profound in the life of a child needing to experience an adoption.

Other candidates for an adoptive dad are an uncle, a granddad, a coach, a teacher...and the list goes on. Anyone, even someone who has never been a father before, can fill the shoes of a father in someone's life if he is a proper fit.

However, it's important to note that this type of substitute relationship shouldn't be forced. It often grows naturally and becomes easier as time passes. Eventually, it becomes a healthy relationship and one that feels safe, encouraging, and like home - the way it should have been all along.

Sadly, many in America don't know what a healthy family looks like. The definition of *"family"* is changing as traditional views of marriage are changing. Family unity is the bedrock of society. When it begins to falter, so does society.

Single moms are special people. I have witnessed sons growing up under their care who are kind, considerate, and high achievers. However, there is still a need for the child to have the positive influence of a father figure in their lives. Without one, where will he draw any experiences to learn from when he himself becomes a father?

As the dad of three daughters, I recognize the daddy/daughter relationship is one of the strongest and most important in shaping them mentally, morally, and spiritually. In a sense, it keeps them healthy, growing their self-esteem and self-worth.

After years of counseling women as a family therapist, chaplain, and pastor, I have seen too often the negative effects of an absent dad in a daughter's life. It's not just like a hole in her heart; it's an aching for someone to fill it.

We all need and long to be loved. Yet, when we aren't vocally hearing someone expressing love to us, a love deficit can grow. (Notice I said *vocally*, for some think that love should be understood through provision of food, shelter, etc., *only*. This is far from the truth - and reality.)

When someone isn't daily being filled with positives, one will eventually drain empty from the negatives they are experiencing.

(See the "love bucket" picture to help you visually understand this.)

When someone knows they *are* loved, they can be filled to the brim with praise, presence, provision, and protection. Even if a hole of disappointment with a father (for example) forms in a relationship, they aren't drained empty. There is always a hope for patching things up.

When someone truly knows they are loved, they know that no matter what they do, there will always be positives of love to draw from. They believe they are loved because they *are*.

However, when someone *isn't* loved as they should be, emptiness creeps in and cracks their love bucket. Now they see themselves for what they experience - disregarded, criticized, withholding of solid relationships, and jeopardized of all care.

So, when disappointment takes place in a relationship, even when love is occasionally poured into their bucket, it leaks right out, draining all hope of love from staying around for very long.

If you find yourself in this situation, *I am very sorry*! You might feel like you are at the bottom of your bucket - unseen and unknown. You might not even know where to begin to conceptualize what it's like to draw any love in your life that lasts.

Sadly, one can (and often does) go looking for love in all the wrong places because of this. Such emptiness in one's life can lead to strings of broken relationships, teen pregnancy, and even marriages without a solid base.

Thankfully, there is a Heavenly Father who is willing to fill our love bucket if we choose to receive these regular fillings.

LOVE BUCKET

FILLS:		EMPTIES:
Praise		Criticism
Presense		Absence
Provision		Withholding
Protection		Jeopardy

STEPFATHER

Accepting the role of a stepfather comes with its own set of challenges. The title itself implies a mother and her children have already experienced separation, divorce, or death. The family unit may still be tip-toeing around the emotional challenges of hurt, anger, or loss. In reality, this may never get better.

Here is how Stephan B. Poulter defines this type of stand-in dad:

"The term stepfather is a legal term, but in a relational context, the prefix step has little bearing on a man's true effectiveness as a father."[11]

Just as a dad being **biological** doesn't automatically define him as good, a *stepfather* cannot automatically bridge the gap of fatherlessness with his new title. More than likely, he never will, even with his best efforts and intentions in mind.

For example, a stepfather may long to be called *"Father"* or *"Dad"* by his stepchildren. However, this isn't a topic to force. Doing so will only lead to further anger (*"You are not my father/mother!"*). It's not unusual for children to call any step-parent by their first name. A stepfather must demonstrate patience and wisdom to gain trust.

A wise word:

"Do not rush into *step-fathering.*"[12]

Building the foundation of a healthy marriage is the key in successful parenting. You and your spouse will need time to get away to talk and develop a unified front on how to approach parenting. You will need to reason together to present a sense of teamwork in approaching daily challenges. One of those challenges will be who will take the lead when discipline is necessary in the parenting process.

A stepfather should encourage the children to have an ongoing relationship with their biological father if possible.

One of my favorite TV commercials features a stepfather and his stepdaughter. As she is growing up, she calls him by his first name.

Years later on her wedding day, her loving stepfather says to her before the wedding:

"You are beautiful."

She smiles and says to him for the first time:

"Thanks, Dad."

I tear up every time I hear her say those words. This stepfather invested years in earning her trust and her love, to finally hear her say *"Thanks, Dad."*

Being a stepfather can be as rich and meaningful as being a natural father. It will take time, and may begin with the establishment of mutual respect and trust. The development of love will come through putting one's self aside and being other person centered.

GRANDDAD

The nuclear family is composed of father, mother, and children. However, a growing number of children do not have the privilege of interaction with their extended family. An extended family is an outgrowth of the nuclear family which includes grandparents, cousins, aunts, uncles, as well as other relatives.

A granddad is a central person in the extended family. Some even refer to him as the patriarch of the family. Due to the breakdown in the nuclear family today, many children will never experience the benefit of being loved and nurtured by a granddad.

Being a granddad is so much more than just a name. He is a repository of facts and experiences. After growing up with a younger brother, I loved seeing my dad holding my daughters and interacting with them. He told them stories that seemed to get embellished in time. Actually, I would listen to him talking with them and learn new things about him I'd never heard before.

My dad made it through the difficult days of the Great Depression. He served in the Army in WWII and was a prisoner of war in Germany. Yet, these stories were rarely shared to me as a son. It wasn't until my children started asking him questions that he started talking. They gave him the opportunity and the right time to pass down the oral tradition of storytelling.

Granddads are not disciplinarians. Neither are they to contradict Mom and Dad's instructions. Granddad teaches by talking about their lives.

There is an element of wisdom gained through the years of his life. In the Bible it is called *"a gift from God"* (James 1:3). If you have ever encountered a granddad with wisdom, you are indeed blessed.

However, words spoken in quantity do not express more than words spoken with quality. Wisdom is also revealed through limited words spoken, though each word that is spoken is pregnant with meaning.

When I served on church governing boards, "young

101

bucks" (or young men) would go *on and on* in board meetings. Finally, the wise, older sage in the room would speak just a few words that brought everything into focus. Wisdom goes beyond just being intelligent. It can be described as discernment or prudence.

Let children ask whatever questions they want to ask. A granddad has time to listen and respond in a way that makes each question valid.

So how does a granddad truly impact his grandkids? Being present is essential.

Sometimes kids just want to crawl up on your lap or receive a big hug. Show up at their sporting event or milestone in their life. Speak well of their mom and dad and share stories about when they were kids.

Teach them how to hunt, fish, or work on cars. Engage in the skills they are interested in which they can pass down to the next generation. Take time to break out the picture albums of the past. It's true that a picture does speak a thousand words.

Even now I am grateful for my grandads. Thank you, Granddad Hussey and Granddad Cockman. My mind is filled with memories of each of you. I can still see your faces, sun-weathered from farming the land. I can still smell the earth on your overalls.

DISCUSSION QUESTIONS:

1. How would you describe your relationship with your father/dad during your childhood?

2. Did you have an adoptive dad in your life?

3. Do you have unresolved father issues? How did you begin to resolve these issues?

4. I wish my father/ dad would have _____.

5. How did a granddad influence your life?

NOTES:

_____

_____

_____

_____

_____

_____

_____

_____

_____

_____

_____

_____

_____

_____

_____

_____

_____

_____

CHAPTER 7:

Forever Father

As a child, some of my first mental pictures of God were those of a grandfather figure with a white beard, floating in the clouds. I think I was influenced by the painting I viewed which attempted to depict God in human form.

The son of God (Jesus) began what we know as "The Lord's Prayer" with these words:

"Our Father in heaven…"

Jesus could have said *my* Father; however, He said *our* Father.

Maybe your view of the Heavenly Father is a being that is distant from His creation and has no desire to have an ongoing relationship? The reality is that God is ever present, and a relationship with Him is ours to enter into.

KNOWING GOD ON A RELATIONAL BASIS

A number of our earthly father issues could be resolved if we knew God as our Heavenly Father on a relational level. As Psalm 68:5 () declares:

"A father to the fatherless, a defender of widows, is God in his holy dwelling."

Martyn Lloyd Jones stated: "The eternal everlasting God has become our Father and the moment we realize that, it transforms everything."[13]

A seminary professor was vacationing with his wife in Gatlinburg, TN. One morning, when they had ordered breakfast and were waiting for their food, they noticed a distinguished looking man with white hair visiting with the restaurant guests. The professor leaned over and whispered to his wife, *"I hope he isn't coming over here."* But sure enough, the man did come over to their table.

"Where are you folks from?"

"Oklahoma," they answered."

"Great to have you here in Tennessee," the stranger said. *"What do you do for a living?"*

"I teach at a seminary," the professor replied.

"Oh, you teach preachers how to preach, do you? Well,

I've got a great story for you."

The professor groaned and thought to himself, *"Great...
just what I need...another preacher story!"*

The man continued:

*"See that mountain over there? Not far from the base
of that mountain, there was a boy born to an unwed mother.
He had a hard time growing up, because every place he
went, he was always asked the same question, 'Hey boy,
who's your daddy?'*

*He would hide at recess and lunch time from other
students. He would avoid going into stores because that
question hurt him.*

*When he was about 12 years old, a new preacher came
to his church. He would always go in late and slip out
early to avoid hearing the question.*

*One day, the new preacher said the benediction so fast
that he got caught and had to walk out with the crowd. Just
about the time he got to the back door, the new preacher, not
knowing anything about him, put his hand on his shoulder
and asked him, 'So, who's your daddy?'*

*The preacher sensed the situation and responded, 'Wait
a minute. I know who you are. I see the family resemblance
now; you are a child of God.'*

With that, the boy smiled for the first time in a long time

107

and walked out the door a changed person. He was never the same again. Whenever anybody asked him, 'Who's your daddy? he'd just tell them, 'I am a child of God.'"

The distinguished gentlemen got up from the table and said, *"Isn't that a great story?"* The professor responded that it was a great story.

As the man turned to leave, he said:

"You know, if that new preacher hadn't told me that I was one of God's children I probably never would have amounted to anything."

As he walked away the professor and his wife were stunned. He called the waitress over and asked her, *"Do you know who that man was…the one who just left that was sitting at our table?"*

The waitress grinned and said, *"Of course. Everybody here knows him. That's Ben Hooper. He's the governor of Tennessee."*[14]

ANNOUNCEMENT:

You are a child of God; you are one of God's crowning creations. You have a Heavenly Father who will never leave you. He is not disinterested, but knows how many hairs are on your head (Matthew 10:26-31). Your life is not without meaning or without purpose (Jeremiah 29:11).

No matter your earthly father experiences, you have an ever-present Heavenly Father who loves you with an everlasting love.

How do I experience this relationship?

Well, we need to get to know Him by:

1. reading about Him in the Bible,

2. talking to Him through prayer,

3. and believing in His Son.

GOD AS FATHER

"Yet for us there is but one God, the Father, from whom all things came and for whom we live; and there is but one Lord, Jesus Christ, through whom all things came and through whom we live" (I Corinthians 8:6).

God is revealed in three persons - Father, Son, and Holy Spirit. Jesus came to earth to reveal the person of God and demonstrate His love for His crowning creation.

"Phillip said, 'Lord, show us the Father and that will be enough for us.' Jesus answered: 'Don't you know me, Phillip, even after I have been among you for such a long time? Anyone who has seen me has seen the Father. How can you say, "show us the Father?"

109

*Don't you believe that I am in the father, and
that the father is in Me?'" (John 14:8-10IV).*

God's Son is the second person of the Trinity, who took
on bodily form and lived among us to reveal what God is
like. Many perceive God as a punisher. Jesus demonstrated
God's love for humanity. Jesus fed the hungry, healed the
sick, and taught how to have a relationship with the Father.
Jesus' teaching is God's teaching. Jesus' works are God's
works. They are not two gods, but one God manifested in
three persons.

God is also revealed in the person of the Holy Spirit.
The Holy Spirit is not a mythological mist that permeates
the universe, but is a living person. The Spirit is operative
throughout the Bible.

The Holy Spirit was at work in creation. He came upon
prophets and others for special occasions in Old Testament
days.

Today the Holy Spirit empowers God's children to
communicate to others about the birth, death, resurrection
and return of Christ. He also leads us and confirms to us we
are indeed children of God.

Every person of the trinity compliments the other.

GOD AS FATHER IN THE OLD TESTAMENT

In the Old Testament God is often referred to as *Yahweh* which means "*to be.*" If you've ever read through the pages of the Old Testament, you may have (at times) had a difficult time seeing a loving Heavenly Father. Some believe God in the Old Testament is more of a God of wrath than the caring Father revealed in the New Testament.

So the question arises:

Does God change from the Old Testament to the New Testament?

The quick answer is no. One of the attributes of God is that He never changes.

God also does not improve over time; He is perfect. God does not grow more in love with humanity; His love is eternal, everlasting, and unconditional. The God of the Old Testament is the same God of the New Testament.

In the Old Testament there was a special covenant relationship with Israel. However, in the New Testament God reveals himself to all humanity in and through His Son.

Jesus was present in the Old Testament:

"In the beginning was the Word, and the Word was with God, and the Word was God.

He was with God in the beginning" (John 1:1-2).

There are some who feel more comfortable viewing God as creator rather than Father in the Old Testament. This can arise from a distant relationship with their earthly father which is transferred onto the Heavenly Father.

Father God is present in the Old Testament. He entered into a special relationship with the nation of Israel. He provided for His children and protected them in their journey to the Promised Land. As Psalm 103:13 says:

"As a father has compassion on his children, so the Lord has compassion on those who fear him..."

God also reveals Himself as Father in Exodus 4:22-23:

"Then say to Pharaoh, 'This is what the Lord says: Israel is my firstborn son, and I told you, Let my son go, so he may worship me. But you refused to let him go'..."

Also, in Isaiah 63:17:

"But you are our Father, though Abraham doesn't know us or Israel acknowledges us: you, O Lord, are our Father, our Redeemer from old is your name."

Although there was a special Fatherly relationship with His chosen people, God as creator is present for *all* humanity in the Old Testament. This consistent truth becomes especially clear in the New Testament when God includes His own Son in the story.

GOD AS FATHER
IN THE NEW TESTAMENT

In the New Testament Jesus takes on skin and lives among us. He is a reflection of the Father. He wants to share His relationship with His Father with us.

Our relationship with God is one of adoption. As Romans 8:15says:

"For you did not receive a spirit that makes you a slave again to fear, but you received the Spirit of sonship (adoption) And by him we cry, Abba, Father."

Sonship in this verse equates with adoption. "*Abba*" is Aramaic for *father*. We are no longer those who only know about God; we now are part of the family:

> "*Consequently, you are no longer foreigners and aliens, but fellow citizens with God's people and members of God's household*" *(Ephesians 2:19).*

Father God initiates the adoption. We did not earn adoption nor do we deserve it, but God by His mercy and grace conveys this eternal blessing. There is nothing flawed about this adoption. We are not secondary sons and daughters, whether of Israel or gentiles. We are *one* in Christ.

I remember times when we would go to family reunions in North Carolina. There was just something special about being with aunts, uncles, cousins, and grandparents. We could see our family resemblances in our shared physical features and mannerisms.

In our Heavenly Father's family, there is a resemblance. There is a oneness in Christ that cannot be fully conveyed in words. There is a special family feeling when we join together in worship. It is a family that cannot be permanently separated by death, because we have eternal life through Christ.

At funerals I conducted, I would often emphasize that this was not a final goodbye, but a time to acknowledge that we would see fellow believers again.

Before my father died, he asked me:

"Son, do you think we will know each other in heaven?"

I assured him through my biblical readings that we *would* know each other. I assured him that in heaven time was not a limiting factor, and before he knew it, I would be there. He replied:

"Son, I will be looking for you."

This is all possible because of the Heavenly Father's gift of His Son. Jesus shared with His disciples: "And if I go and prepare a place for you, I will come back and take you to be with me so that you also may be where I am" (John 14:3).

In Christ we bear the family likeness, where once we were outside, wandering, lost not feeling a part of anything. Our new life in Christ is a call to be like Christ, so others might know we are sons and daughters of a living Father and God.

I Corinthians 8:6:

> *"Yet for us here is but one God, the Father, from whom all things came and for whom we live; and there is but one Lord, Jesus Christ, through whom all things came and through whom we live."*

AN UNOBSTRUCTED VIEW OF THE FATHER

DISCUSSION QUESTIONS:

1. What mental picture of God did you have as a child?

2. How do you get to know the Heavenly Father?

3. What three persons does God reveal Himself in?

4. How do you describe your relationship with God now?

5. Is there a difference between God in the O.T and God in the N.T?

NOTES:

_____

_____

_____

_____

_____

_____

_____

_____

_____

_____

_____

_____

_____

_____

_____

_____

_____

CHAPTER 8:

God As Friend

Some might question whether an infinite being, who is the creator, can be a friend to finite beings. Below are two ways God reveals His choice to be close to His crowning creation:

1. He communicates with us.

"But the Lord God called to the man,
Where are you?'" (Genesis 3:9).

God knew where Adam and Eve's hiding places were, but He was looking for them to openly communicate with Him. In this verse, we find God initiates the conversation (already knowing what the subject was).

2. He created us in His image.

"So God created man in His own image, in the
image of God he created him; male and female he
created them" (Genesis 1:26).

Man was created in the image of God. Since God is not flesh but spirit, this does mean man was made in the image of God in a physical sense. The image of God is a reflection of who God is in a spiritual sense. Because God is holy, man is called to be holy. Because God is loving and kind, man is called to be loving and kind.

Who then (if anyone) is reflective of the perfect image of God?

In Colossians 1:15, the Apostle Paul reminds us that Jesus is *"the image of the invisible God."* Only Jesus. Only the Son is the embodiment of the Father. (This was a huge, life-changing reality for Paul, a former murderer of Christians. He was once an enemy of God, but in his surrender to God's authority, he even found friendship with Him.)

FRIEND OF GOD

We demonstrate friendship with Father God in living in the right relationship with Him. Friendship with God is not exclusive; He seeks a friendship with all of humanity.

Israel Houghton has a song entitled: "Friend of God" which declares a mutual friendship between God and him. It displays a relationship that is open and loving. If you have not heard this song, I encourage you to listen to it.

FRIENDSHIP INVOLVES OBEDIENCE

Obedience is a choice to follow the principles that are found in the Bible. Being a friend of God does not lessen His position of authority as our sovereign, but is reflective of a relational aspect, one of friendship. We worship Him, but we can also call Him friend.

In obeying Jesus, we obey the Father. Jesus said:

> *"You are my friends if you do what I command. I no longer call you servants, because a servant does not know his master's business. Instead, I have called you friends, for everything that I learned from my Father I have made known to you. You did not choose me, but I chose you to go and bear fruit-fruit that will last. Then the Father will give you whatever you ask in my name. This is my command: love each other" (John 15:14-17).*

FRIENDSHIP INVOLVES COMMUNICATION

How do we communicate with our Heavenly Father?

Jesus demonstrates throughout the New Testament the importance of prayer. Prayer is communicating with any one of the three persons of the Trinity. Jesus taught His disciples to pray in what we call "The Lord's Prayer." God is *"Our Father..."* (Matthew 6:9), yet prayer can be an individual conversation with God. We think that prayer is one-sided, our request, our confession, our praise, *but do we pause to listen to how God might respond?*

You may assume that He says one of the following:

"Yes."

"No."

"Wait."

"Change your request."

"You have got to be kidding."

I have lived long enough to know God answers prayers, but not necessarily in my timeframe.

We need to talk with God before we talk with others. Prayer should be our first work. Prayer should not be the last thing we do, after we have tried everything else.

I recall a story where a man had fallen off a ledge and was clinging for life on the cliff's side. He began to cry out, *"Help! Is there anyone up there?"*

After some time, he heard a voice say:

"My son, just let go!"

The man said, *"Who are you?"*

He heard, *"I am God."*

The man thought for a minute and then cried out, *"Is there anyone else up there?"*

The act of prayer is the acknowledgement He *is* there. His response to our request will reflect His sovereignty, His mercy, and His plan for our good and His glory.

Scripture reveals that Abraham was called a friend of God. God referred to him as a friend:

> *"But you, O Israel, my servant, Jacob, who*
> *I have chosen, you descendants of Abraham*
> *my friend" (Isaiah 41:8).*

God, to Abraham. was not a distant deity. God, to Abraham ,was not just an acquaintance.

ABRAHAM WAS ATTENTIVE TO THE VOICE OF GOD

I remember a phrase from a commercial that appeared on television a number of years ago - *"When E.F. Hutton talks, people listen."* I wish this were the case when God speaks. When God spoke, Abraham listened - and Abraham obeyed. Genesis 12:1-9.

ABRAHAM BELIEVED GOD

> *"And the scripture was fulfilled that says,*
> *'Abraham believed God and it was credited*

to him as righteousness, and he was called God's friend'" (James 2:23.).

Abraham's friendship with God was reciprocated with many blessings, one in particular that we share: *"and all peoples on earth will be blessed through you"* (Genesis 12:3b).

DISCUSSION QUESTIONS:

1. Can God be our friend?

2. How has God demonstrated friendship to you?

3. How do you communicate with God?

4. How do we hear from God?

5. Why would some see God as a foe?

NOTES:

_____

_____

_____

_____

_____

_____

_____

_____

_____

_____

_____

_____

_____

_____

_____

_____

_____

_____

CHAPTER 9:

Knowledge of Father God

Most who have had some form of biblical instruction know that God is omniscient, omnipresent, and omnipotent. Simply put, God is all knowing, ever present, and all powerful.

As A.W. Tozer says in his book *The Knowledge of the Holy*:

"The heaviest obligation lying upon the Christian Church today is to purify and elevate her concept of God until it is once more worthy of Him—and of her."[15]

We elevate our understanding of God as we examine His attributes.

Yet in my journey to grow in my knowledge of God, I've come to learn that I will never arrive at a full understanding of God. I am still stuck on God's words to Moses in Exodus 3:14a , "I am that I Am." To me, this reveals that God is absolute and complete within Himself. (*How can the finite fully comprehend the infinite?*) Yet the journey to know more about the Almighty must go on for us to advance spiritually.

ATTRIBUTES OF GOD

We have previously determined God is all knowing, ever present, and all powerful. Here are some additional ways God is known.

1. He is all wise.

*"Oh, the depth of the riches of the wisdom
and knowledge of God! How unsearchable his
judgments, and his paths beyond tracing out!"
Romans 11:33 (NIV).*

We are not all wise. Only God is all wise and all powerful. In His wisdom, He has ordered the universe. In His wisdom, He has a plan for our individual lives. There is no chaos in His wisdom; His wisdom has no limitations. Indeed, it is infinite. Though humanity is not all wise, man can ask God for wisdom, which aids in the growth of our knowledge and understanding. As James 5:1 (NIV) says:

*"If any of you lacks wisdom, he should ask God
who gives generously to all without finding fault,
and it will be given to him."*

2. He does not change.

In Psalm 90:2 (NIV): "Before the mountains were born or you brought forth the earth and the world, from everlasting to everlasting you are God."

I have heard it said that the only one who likes to be changed is a baby. Humanity in general has a fear of change. Yet in this world we seem to be surrounded by change.

In my philosophy class in college, I remember learning that the Greek philosopher Heraclitus is credited with the idea that the only constant in life is change. Nothing remains still, but life is like a river that flows on and on.

When I think about change Psalm 46:10b flashes into my mind:

"Be still and know that I am God..."

God is constant, He is not growing, He is complete. The God of Moses is your God and Father. He has not changed in time, for He exists outside of time's limitations. As Hebrews 13:8 highlights:

"Jesus Christ is the same yesterday and today and forever."

As the Father is immutable, so is the Son. The only exception is that the Son of God took on flesh (and stepped into the limitation of our time for a season) that we might have the opportunity to believe in Him and receive the gift of eternal life.

3. He is holy.

"But just as he who called you is holy, so be holy in all you do; for it is written: 'Be holy, because I am holy'" (I Peter 1:15-16).

Tozer says:

> *"Holy is the way God is. To be holy God does not conform to a standard. He is the standard. He is absolutely holy with an infinite, incomprehensible fullness of purity that is incapable of being other than it is. Because He is holy, all His attributes are holy; that is, whatever we think of as belonging to God must be thought of as holy."*[16]

It is God's will that His children be holy. The third person of the Trinity, the Holy Spirit, is operative in this ongoing process. He becomes resident in our lives after we receive the Son of God, but there must be a growth in grace which takes place through reading, meditating, and studying God's Word. It comes in emptying ourselves of self-focus and fixing our focus on the author and finisher of our faith. It is moving from the residency of the Holy Spirit to the presidency of the Holy Spirit in our lives.

I received Christ into my life when I was a boy in the fourth grade. Yet, it wasn't until years later, in October of 1971 during a revival at Nyack College, that the Spirit took over the presidency in my life. Christian growth does not come in an "instant grits" package. It's progressive. It is a growth in wisdom and holiness.

The constant chanting of heaven that never stops is:

"Holy, holy, holy
Is the Lord God Almighty,
Who was, and is, and is to come"
(Revelation 4:8b).

Holy is the way God is, and some would even say that holiness is His chief attribute. There is an indescribable splendor in His holiness.

4. He is just.

"He is the Rock, his works are perfect, and all his ways are just. A faithful God who does no wrong and who is just" (Deuteronomy 32:4).

Our lives on earth are surrounded with injustice. Some say there are two scales of justice - one for the powerful and the influential, and another set of scales for the poor and defenseless. People who have suffered injustice at the hands of others can become discouraged, embittered, and simply deteriorate through life.

Listen, my friend - God is *just*. I've counseled numerous people throughout the years who languish in thinking they will never receive justice. I usually assure them that God does not settle injustices necessarily in our time frame, but ultimately His justice will prevail.

Jesus too felt the sting of injustice on levels that would have crushed the mighty.

5. He loves you.

Just because God is just, this does not contradict the reality that He *loves*. God's justice provides us a way of pardon through His love. God's justice was met through the sacrifice of His Son. Justice does not preclude forgiveness, but the penalty must be paid.

When Christ was on the cross, he spoke these words in Luke 23:34 :

> *"...Father, forgive them, for they do not know what they are doing."*

Then came these closing words from the cross in John 19:30:

> *"It is finished."*

The Greek word for finished is "tetelestai." It literally means "debt paid in full."

6. He is merciful.

> *In Exodus 34:6: "And He passed in front of Moses, proclaiming, 'The Lord, the Lord, the compassionate and gracious God, slow to anger, abounding in love and faithfulness.'"*

Many picture God, particularly in the Old Testament, as a resident policeman just waiting for someone to break the law so He can dispense justice. Yet, the mercy of God runs throughout the Old Testament. As in Lamentations 3:22-23:

"The steadfast love of the Lord never ceases; his mercies never come to an end; they are new every morning; great is your faithfulness."

In the New Testament, think of the thief on the cross who received mercy in the midst of Christ's agony.

Our heavenly Father is indeed just, yet He is also good and merciful, and His mercy is personally extended to each of us through His Son, 2 Peter 3:9:

"The Lord is not slow in keeping his promise, as some understand slowness. He is patient with you, not wanting anyone to perish, but everyone to come to repentance."

7. He is good.

"Taste and see that the Lord is good; blessed is the man who takes refuge in him."

- Psalm 34:8

His mercy and goodness go hand and hand. As Tozer proclaims:

The goodness of God is that which disposes

Him to be kind, cordial, benevolent, and full of good will toward men He is tenderhearted and of quick sympathy, and His unfailing attitude toward all moral beings is open, frank, and friendly. By His nature He is inclined to bestow blessedness and He takes holy pleasure in the happiness of His people.[17]

8. He is eternal.

"Before the mountains were born or you brought forth the earth and the world, from everlasting to everlasting you are God" Psalm 90:2 (NIV.

God has no beginning and no end. A simple illustration might be a circle. A circle has no beginning; it has no end.

I must admit when I think of eternity, infinite and unending time, a circuit breaker kicks off in my mind. In this finite existence, we have restrictions of time and space. There is "a time to be born,", and there is "a time to die," Ecclesiastes 3:2I. Time plays out on a linear timeline.

Yet, God is active in time and space and He is not limited by either. With this being said, He called on His Son to step into the linear timeline of humanity. He could have left *us* to wander forever in our sin. However, He created a way out through the sacrifice of His Son, so we could be in forever existence with Him.

I have often thought about what that must have felt like for the eternal Word (Jesus), to take on flesh and dwell

KNOWLEDGE OF FATHER GOD

among us, to provide the way to eternal life.

Praise God that human history is linear (ending point) and eternity with God is circular (never ends).

9. He is faithful.

I Corinthians 1:9): "God, who has called you into fellowship with his Son Jesus Christ our Lord, is faithful."

When we think of faithfulness, we might think of marriage vows. Today, too many marriages experience broken fidelity in extramarital affairs. I have counseled those who find that their mate has broken those promises. Oftentimes the pain cannot be expressed in words; it is a heaving of the innermost being - a violation of love and trust. There is no instant solution for this pain. Though forgiveness can be given, the healing of hurt takes as long as it takes.

In Old Testament scripture, God's relationship with Israel is compared to a marriage commitment. Yet, even amidst Israel's infidelity, God was willing to take her back upon the following conditions, in Hosea 14:1-2:

"Return, O Israel, to the Lord your God. Your sins have been your downfall! Take words with you and return to the Lord. Say to him: 'Forgive all our sins and receive us graciously, that we may offer the fruit of our lips.'"

10. He is sovereign.

"Ah, Sovereign Lord, you have made the heavens and the earth by your great power and outstretched arm. Nothing is too hard for you," Jeremiah 32:17.

God is sovereign over all that is and all that is to come. World leaders come and go, but God's rule and reign is eternal.

One of the most powerful rulers of all time was Nebuchadnezzar, the king of Babylon. At that time, Babylon was one of the greatest centers of the ancient Near East.

Yet, Nebuchadnezzar was filled with pride. Listen to his words and how God replies in Daniel 4:30-31:

"Is not this the great Babylon I have built as the royal residence, by my mighty power and for the glory of my majesty?"

"The words were still on his lips when a voice came from heaven. 'This is what is decreed for you, King Nebuchadnezzar:

Your royal authority has been taken from you."

Years later, and after he came to his senses after being stricken with insanity, Nebuchadnezzar said in Daniel 4:34b-35:

His dominion is an eternal dominion;
His kingdom endures from generation to

generation. All the peoples of the earth are regarded as nothing. He does as he pleases with the powers of heaven and the peoples of the earth. No one can hold back his hand or say to him:

"What have you done?"

Too many kings and rulers have viewed themselves as gods. However, trying to hold power is like trying to hold sand in your hands. The sands of human time run out so quickly, as Nebuchadnezzar found out.

In the midst of His sovereignty, God has granted man a free will. He does not rule like a dictator, but chooses in His sovereignty to love us enough to give us free choice. He in love has provided pardon for our rebellion through the gift of His Son. It is our choice to receive or reject this gift of eternal life.

When it comes to God's person, to His promises, He is completely faithful. All the attributes of God are contiguous; they are unified within the circle of oneness.

Experiencing and accepting the reality of God's faithfulness moves us to realize all His promises are true. Our part is to believe. Time and time again in the OT when Israel had strayed from their covenant relationship, God would say, as in Malachi 3:6b :

"Return to Me and I will return to you."

137

This list of God's attributes is not all-inclusive, but remembering them can help us grow in wisdom, knowledge, and understanding of God.

I can hear some of your thoughts:

"Okay, Rick, I appreciate the list of attributes, but what can He do for me in the here and now?"

Friend, God is trustworthy. Observe the many ways you can count on God:

1. He loves you.

The Lord appeared in the past saying:

"I have loved you with an everlasting love; I have drawn you with loving-kindness."

- Jeremiah 31:3

2. He has a plan for your life.

"For I know the plans I have for you," declared, the Lord, "plans to prosper you and not to harm you, plans to give you hope and a future. Then you will call upon me and come and pray to me, and I will listen to you. You will seek me and find me when you seek me with all your heart" Jeremiah 29:11-13)

3. He hears your prayers.

"This is the assurance we have in approaching God: that if we ask anything according to his will, he hears us. And if we know that he hears us—whatever we ask—we know that we have what we asked of him."

- I John 5:14-15 V

4. He provides for you.

"And my God will meet all your needs according to his glorious riches in Christ Jesus."

- Philippians 4:19

6. He makes a way.

"Trust in the Lord with all your heart and lean not on your own understanding; in all your ways acknowledge Him, and He will make your paths straight."

- Proverbs 3:5-6

7. He can make you whole physically and emotionally.

"But I will restore you to health and heal your wounds."

- Jeremiah 30:17

8. He is your protector.

"But the Lord is faithful, and he will strengthen and protect you from the evil one."

- 2 Thessalonians 3:3

9. He gives sleep to those He loves.

"In vain you rise early and stay up late, toiling for food to eat; for He grants sleep to those he loves."

- Psalm 127:2

10. He is a saving God.

"Our God is a God who saves; from the Sovereign Lord comes escape from death."

- Psalm 68:20

The fourth question of the Westminster Shorter Catechism asks:

"What is God?"

The answer is:

"God is a Spirit, infinite, eternal, and unchangeable in His being, wisdom, power, holiness, justice, goodness and truth."

Knowing God and experiencing Him as our Heavenly Father, our Forever Father, is essential in living life to the fullest now and for all eternity.

J.I. Packer, in his historic book *Knowing God,* concluded:

"What were we made for? *To know God.* What aim should we set ourselves in life? To know God. What is the 'eternal life' that Jesus gives? Knowledge of God..."[18] It is essential that we know God as our Forever Father. To know Him as Father we first know His Son as our Savior. We are adopted into the family of God as a gift of God's *R*iches *A*t *C*hrist's *E*xpense.

DISCUSSION QUESTIONS:

1. How do we elevate our understanding of God?

2. Does God change?

3. Can God be both loving and just?

4. What are some ways you can count on God?

5. Can God heal damaged emotions?

NOTES:

_____

_____

_____

_____

_____

_____

_____

_____

_____

_____

_____

_____

_____

_____

_____

_____

_____

_____

_____

_____

CHAPTER 10:

Future Father

*What does the role of the Heavenly Father and the
role of an earthly father look like in the future?*

ETERNAL EXISTENCE

I remember seeing the cover of *Time*, a weekly
news magazine, in April of 1966. It was the first time the
magazine posted a cover without a picture. The background
was black and in red lettering this question was asked, *"Is
God Dead?" The article evoked many angry sermons and
3,421 letters (at the time 97% of Americans believed in
God)*[19] Today, with 74 % of Americans saying they believe
in God, the question about where God is (and if God is)
continues to grow.

Some believe that God never existed. In this theory,
everything we see and experience around us simply evolved
without any divine orchestration. This is like saying a wind
blew through a salvage yard and a jet plane was constructed.

This leads to more questions. So then, *"Where did the wind come from?"* and *"Where did the salvage yard come from?"*

The Apostle Paul provides an alternative view:

> *"For since the creation of the world God's invisible qualities - His eternal power and divine nature have been clearly seen, being understood from what has been made, so that men are without excuse."*
>
> **- Romans 1:20**

Paul validates God as an eternal being, powerful, divine in nature, and visible through His creation. He was not created, but created out of *"ex nihilo"* (Latin) or "nothing" that now exists. So, men are without excuse who question His existence.

God is known through His creation, through His Word, through His Son. Knowing God is foundational. It is not just knowing about God; our call is to know Him relationally. In knowing Him one finds purpose, meaning, and hope eternally.

We can declare:

I am a child of God.

He is my Father forever.

Heaven is my everlasting home.

CONSISTENT HEAVENLY FATHER?

Things all around us are evolving or devolving. Change seems to be a constant in this world. People question if there are any absolutes in this age of relativism. Some feel that they are living in quicksand...there is no solid ground to stand on.

The reassuring news is that the one, true God of the past is the same God of the present and the future. He has no beginning. He has no end. He is eternally the same. He was, He is, and He is to come. See Revelation 1:8. He is not evolving or devolving, but He is the *"I am."*

God's love for His crowning creation, man, is an everlasting love. It is not contingent on us being good or being bad. His love is constant. His love is freely extended to us. But, for us to experience this love, we must transfer our trust to Him, and turn from our sin through a relationship with His Son.

Paul sums it up in his letter to the church at Ephesus:

> *"For it is by grace you have been saved, through faith and this not from ourselves, it is the gift of God not by works, so that no one can boast."*

- Ephesians 2:8-9

The Apostles Creed has been a part of church liturgy for centuries (it is dated no later than the fourth century).

It begins with the foundation of faith in an eternal God, Father, and creator. So, man's free will response in faith is, *"I believe."*

APOSTLES CREED

I believe in God, the Father almighty,
creator of heaven and earth.

I believe in Jesus Christ, his only Son, our Lord,
who was conceived by the Holy Spirit
and born of the virgin Mary.
He suffered under Pontius Pilate,
was crucified, died, and was buried;
he descended to hell.
The third day he rose again from the dead.
He ascended to heaven
and is seated at the right hand of God the Father
almighty.
From there he will come to judge the living and the dead.

I believe in the Holy Spirit,
the holy catholic* church,
the communion of saints,
the forgiveness of sins,
the resurrection of the body,
and the life everlasting. Amen.

(* the true Christian church of all times and places)

CHANGING EARTHLY FATHER?

We have established the fact that our Heavenly Father does not change. He is the sure foundation of our faith; He is our Forever Father. He is never absent, but ever present as our provider, protector, and sovereign.

Earthly fathers can change, and hopefully do over their lifetime, for the better. Yet, a dad is not perfect like the Heavenly Father, but a man in process. A dad can be absent in numerous ways. He can only protect so much. He can only lead so long.

I've heard it said, *"You may not be able to do anything about our ancestors, but you can do something about your descendants."* It is never too late to move forward in the process of aiming to become a more effective father.

The Heavenly Father has created the family as the superglue that holds any civilization together. Without this foundation of family, once great nations turn into the sand which archeologists sift through.

HOW FATHERS LEAD THEIR FAMILIES

1. By Loving.

"Husbands love your wives, just as Christ loved the church and gave himself up for her."

- Ephesians 5:22

149

I often share with a husband that one of your greatest investments in life is to love your wife. For every ounce of love, you give she has the ability to return *two*. My simple definition of love is *"to be other person centered."*

Children feel a greater sense of security when they know their dad and mom love each other. There are some days when you won't feel like loving your mate, but you will need to make the choice to love your mate. Love goes beyond feeling; it is a choice.

2. By transparency.

Forget the macho statement, *"Real men don't show emotion."*

Sadly, boys can be raised with what I call the *"suck it up mentality."* They are taught to internalize hurt, anxiety, fears, and failures because if they express them it shows weakness. Yet, some of the most emotionally transparent males I've ever met are those who were raised by single moms. Most of these moms give their sons the freedom to talk it out instead of holding it in.

In marital counseling, many times the wife will talk a mile a minute. Women find emotional release through talking. The problem is that "Bubba" (her husband) will sit there in silence. During such sessions I would gently ask the wife not to speak, but give Bubba time to respond. Sometimes it seemed like an eternity before he'd talk. On occasion I would have to prompt him by asking questions that could not be answered with one-word responses. There were even times I would have him point to a word on a sheet describing how he was feeling. After he would "talk," I would then glance at the wife, who was shocked at the depth of feeling coming out of him (when she assumed he never had a deep thought). He did, he just wasn't able to express it or be heard.

Dad...it's okay to be yourself in front of those you love, to let them know what's on your mind and in your heart. They are longing to hear your story. They will be more willing to express what's on their hearts if you will be real.

For this to happen, you will also need to take time to listen to them. I remember one night one of my young daughters was standing beside me talking a mile a minute. I was doing my male thing; I was watching TV. I would grunt on occasion, pretending I was listening, but she kept on with machine fire verbiage. Finally, I muted the TV and looked her directly in her eyes. When she knew she had my undivided attention she was able to communicate her need in a few sentences.

Dad, time and transparency are worth the investment. Who knows, you might be training a future world changer! Don't let your damaged past infect the present generation.

Better yet, as you find greater transparency in your relationship with the Heavenly Father, you will find greater abilities to live and lead by example. Our communication with our children will grow richer and deeper.

Then, you will be moved to ask questions like, *"When you grow up, what do you want to become?"* Remember, many of the definitions of success in secular life are temporary, unfulfilling, and selfish. It's not the things we leave to our children that are most important (possessions), but it's the modeled pieces of life (purposes) that we can help guide them through this perilous journey called *life*.

3. By Example.

I remember seeing a cartoon which pictured a wild mob of people running in all different directions. It was a chaotic scene. There was a man walking behind the group. Someone asked him, *"Who are you?"* to which he responded, *"I am their leader."* The cartoon ended with this saying, "He who thinks he is a leader, and has no followers, is just taking a walk."

The world's view of a leader is *"one who commands/ demands."* However, I like to think of a leader as one I choose to follow. A leader does not demand respect; they earn respect through living a life that demonstrates a genuine concern for those under their care. A leader provides an example that will elevate the lives of those who choose to follow his/her leadership. A leader does not seek to cling to power, but empowers others to excel, and prepares another to pick up his/her mantle of leadership.

Jesus was such a leader. His words to his disciples also

drew me to follow him. As Jesus said in Matthew 4:19, "Come, follow me, and I will make you fishers of men."

Dad, I hear your thoughts. *"I am not a leader. I don't want to be a leader."* Well, sometimes we don't choose leadership, it chooses us. Being a father is a call to leadership; it's one of the most important titles a man can have. It's a servant leadership role that develops in an atmosphere of love, patience, and trust. As Abraham Lincoln said, *"No man stands taller than when he stoops to help a child."*

The words a father teaches are important, but we must remember when the children are grown, they are more likely to follow your example than your words. Fathering is not a call to perfection, but a process that shapes one in becoming an effective father.

4. By facing challenges.

"The truth is that the culture has been waging war on fathers and sons for a half century, maybe more. Too many young males have lost their way, and not just males from fatherless homes."[20]

Fathers have faced challenges from the beginning of time. But today in our quest to make life easier through advanced technology and conveniences, we have sacrificed family time, honest communication, and marital fidelity to the spirit of the age. The family is faltering. Family is God's creation; it's the fabric that holds any society together. From any perspective, spiritual or secular, the family continues to unravel.

Fathers today and in the future will need to deal with the fear factor. Economic challenges can turn the strongest man into a person full of fear. All the *"What if..."* questions keep one awake at night running all the scenarios.

In the Lord's Prayer (reference), we have learned the joy of saying together *"Our Father."* This prayer also simply asks, *"Give us this day our daily bread."* I have learned that life is lived day by day in dependency on the divine.

Dad, we need to rest in our Heavenly Father as protector and provider as well as trust Him to be true to His promises. King David shares some great news:

> *"I was young and now I am old, yet I have never seen the righteous forsaken or their children begging for bread."* -
> **Psalm 37:25**

Today we need men of courage amidst days of uncertainty. Moses mentored Joshua to pick up his mantle of leadership. When Moses died, these are the words the Heavenly Father brought to Joshua:

> *No one will be able to stand up against you all the days of yourMoses, so I will be with you; I will never leave you or forsake you. Be strong and courageous, because you will lead these people to inherit the land, I swore*

*to their forefathers to give them. Be strong
and very courageous. Be careful to obey all
the law my servant Moses gave you; do not
turn from it let this book of the law depart
from our mouth; meditate on it day and night,
so that you may be careful to do everything
written in it. Then you will be prosperous and
successful. Have I not commanded you: be
strong and courageous, do not be terrified;
do not be discouraged, for the Lord your God
will be with you wherever you go."*

- Joshua 1:5-9

5. By asking for forgiveness.

There are occasions when a dad just gets it wrong.
It could be accusing a child of doing something to later
find out the child was completely innocent. During these
times, there is an important decision to be made. *Will pride
prevent you from acknowledging the wrong? Will you man
up and ask the child for forgiveness?*

I have learned that children are genuine and are quick
in offering forgiveness. It's precious and humbling to hear
the words, *"Daddy, I forgive you."* How many of us still
bear the scars of being falsely accused and punished for
something we did not do? If you bear these scars, ask your
Heavenly Father to heal those hurts.

In simple terms, *"Let go and let God."* Healing may
not be instant, but it will be a process. However, there will
come a time in the process where the emotional pain will

no longer plague you. It will become like a fading picture in your mind.

6. By being responsible.

If your child asks for help on a project, or the repair of a broken bike, let them know that you have heard their request by telling them when you hope to help. Provide an example of the importance of vocalizing what you heard and giving a timeframe when you will help. (Women have shared with me that when they ask their husband to complete a task he usually puts it off.) Also, make it a priority to see that commitment to that task completed.

From a male perspective, here is how it often goes:

Wife:

> *"Honey, the handle lock on the back door is broken, will you fix it?"*

The husband (says to himself):

> *"I will go by the hardware store Friday and pick up a new door knob."*

The problem is, he has said this to himself and his wife doesn't hear a word come out of his mouth.

So, let's suppose this happened on a Monday. By Wednesday the *wife* says:

> *"Honey, are you going to fix the door knob?"*

The husband (says to himself), *"I'm going to do it Friday."*

Again, the wife doesn't hear anything come out of his mouth.

By Thursday, *the wife* in a raised voice (now frustrated) says:

"Are you ever going to fix that door knob?!"

The husband (again to himself says):

"Nag, nag, nag. I'm going to put it off 'til I am good and ready."

Again, the wife didn't hear a word out of his mouth.

Although this is a marital example, it's important to demonstrate responsibility in hearing requests and vocally responding to requests by providing a timeframe. Being responsible will provide an example to your children of the importance of being responsible in life. We need to put aside self-interest, and sacrifice for the benefit of others.

7. By investing time.

Families continue to fracture across America because of growing demands on our time and energy in a multitude of areas.

We try to justify the lack of time with family by rationalizing that it is not the length of time we spend together, but the quality of time we spend together. So we try to pack quality time into vacations and weekends. These planned times are great; however, how we spend our time reflects our priorities in life.

Spending more frequent time together provides greater opportunities to make memories and shape lives. Making memories can be as simple as inviting your child to go with you as you run errands. You will be amazed by the questions they will ask. Never underestimate the power of time together.

ROLES IN THE PAST

In the past, the father...

1. ...was the sole breadwinner in the family.
2. ...was the disciplinarian.
3. ...would give orders without input from others. (This was and is not a good idea.)

ROLES IN THE FUTURE

Today, in approximately 48% of families, both husband and wife are employed. It's not unusual for the wife's earning power to be greater than her husband's. A woman's earning power has tripled over the past fifty years (Pew Research Center).

Today there are a growing number of stay-at-home

fathers, whose identity is not in being the sole breadwinner, but being a nurturer and caregiver. Stay-at-home dads do voice their struggle with a lack of support and feeling alone.

The reasons for a growing number of stay-at-home dads are many. One primary reason is the rising cost of child care. By the time you factor in the cost, as well as additional transportation, meals out, etc., it is a savings for one to stay at home with the kids. There are a greater number of parents who are working at home, which affords more time to be present and available to their children. Companies are also becoming more sensitive to family leave for a variety of reasons.

Parenting is moving more and more to be seen as a team effort versus roles that can be stereotypical. In other words, a dad can do dishes too. Yes, a wife can cut the grass. There is a greater freedom to ask for help when one is facing overload.

Husbands and wives should work together in disciplining children. Children really are adept at pitting parents against one another and using a "divide and conquer" mentality in trying to avoid any disciplinary measures. Discipline is an individualized matter.

All children do not respond to just one form of discipline. My brother was so tender-hearted that all my parents had to do was give him a stern look to bring about change. Discipline must also be issued from a heart of love and concern, never from anger and frustration.

You may have heard the phrase, *"Children are to be seen and not heard."* There was a day when the father spoke and there was no further discussion. However, anger is not an effective tool for men. Anger is the antithesis of love. Anger cuts off effective communication. As Christian men, we are called to speak truth in love.

Making time for family talks can also be a good way to communicate. It's perfectly fine to give others time to ask questions and share their input. Remember, you can be right on a matter, but wrong in cutting off others from expressing their opinions. Yes, there are times when a leader must make the hard decisions, but that might also mean beginning a conversation with listening.

Today, an added challenge also arises because of the increase of single fathers. In the past, single fatherhood was rare. Today we are seeing an increasing number of households led by single fathers. I believe this percentage will continue to rise in the future.

Of course, there are challenges for both the single dad and the single mom. Yet, a dad can face specific issues such as:

- …being less likely to ask for help.

- …being the dad of maturing teens (lacking nurturing abilities).

- ...being the breadwinner (with limited time for the household).

- ...being overwhelmed with the emotional impact of divorce.

A single dad and his children can benefit from the mother's involvement *if* she is willing to be positively involved. Sadly, I have known divorced couples who get along better after their marriage has ended. Regardless, both adults need to put aside their anger and hurt against one another for the benefit of love and the nurture of their children.

Even in brokenness, and especially with God as the center of it all, Father God can make new earthly dads. Yes, there is work to be done, but with full reliance on the Heavenly Father, the best role model there is, there *is* hope for homes today.

DISCUSSION QUESTIONS:

1. What does being a child of God mean to you?

2. How has God shown Himself consistent in your life?

3. Have you seen changes over time in your earthly father?

4. What type of example did your earthly father provide?

5. How did your earthly father face challenges?

NOTES:

THIS EARTHLY FATHER'S FINAL THOUGHTS

What does the future hold? Only our Heavenly Father knows.

Yet, we can rest confident in the fact that He is the same in His love for His crowning creation - past, present, *and* future. We know that He has a plan to prosper us and that He will never leave us or forsake us. Even in the absence of a biological earthly father, our Heavenly Father can provide men to fill in the void which one has left.

Dad, there's always time to change. Make the choice with the Heavenly Father's help to be an effective father *today*.

For those whose father is absent, please remember:

"BIG DAD will always be with you,

even when Little Dad isn't around.

PRAYER:

Our Heavenly Father,

Thank You for creating us in Your image, and placing us as head over all earthly creation. Abba, thank You for demonstrating Your love for us in the midst of our lostness, by giving us Your Son as a sacrifice for our sins. Heavenly Father, grant our earthly fathers the wisdom to lead and to love those under their care.

Amen

Epilogue

Thank you for journeying with me in taking *An Unobstructed View Of The Father* (*On Earth and in Heaven*).

Maybe you have discovered (*for the first time*) that the Heavenly Father loves you and has a desire to have a relationship with you (*even though you have distanced yourself from Him*). Entering into a relationship with Him means not just acknowledging that He exists, but it is deciding to know Him personally. He loves us enough to leave this choice to us, to enter into an eternal relationship with Him - even when He is knocking at our heart's door to do so. When He calls, it's best to listen and respond.

Jesus is a pure reflection of His Father, and His earthly life demonstrated God's way to a restored relationship. That way centers around Jesus dying on a Roman cross to pay for our sins. Sin is an offense against an infinite being; it is choosing our way versus His way and will, and requires an infinite and pure sacrifice for our sins.

The key to a relationship with the Heavenly Father is *faith*, faith in the person and works of Jesus. Faith is transferring one's trust to Jesus' person and works. Once that relationship is established through faith and turning from sin, one becomes a member of the forever family of God.

Life just goes better with knowing God personally. It also has a positive influence on our earthly relationships.

With God as your prime Father, father absenteeism can now be addressed head on, now that you have a never-ending assurance of a present Heavenly Father who will always be there.

The generational curses passed down can end.

A new generation can begin.

Our Heavenly Father can help you in breaking those chains and starting anew.

ADDITIONAL RESOURCES

Lawrence Jones, *American Man*
(New York: Center Street, 2023).

Josh Hawley, *Manhood* (Regnery Publishing, 2023).

A Local Church

Counselor/Therapist

https://bibleproject.com/

https://fathers.com/

http://www.ourfatherless.org

https://fatheringtogether.org/

Endnotes

1. A.W. Tozer, *The Knowledge of the Holy* (Harper and Row, 1961), 35.

2. Lawrence Jones, *American Man* (New York: Center Street, 2023), 45.

3. Josh Hawley, *Manhood* (Regnery Publishing, 2023), page 90.

4. National Fatherhood Initiative, *"Statistics Don't Lie: Fathers Matter,"* 2022, https://fatherhood.org/father-absence-statistic.

5. Henry B. Biller, and Robert J. Trotter, *The Father Factor*, (Pocket Books 1994), 230.

6. Ted W. Engstrom. *The Fine Art of Mentoring* (Wolgemuth & Hyatt, Publisher Inc., Brentwood, Tennessee, 1989), 13.

7. C.S. Lewis, *The Abolition of Man* (New York: Macmillian, 1947), 101.

8. Donald Joy, *Unfinished Business* (Wheaton IL: Victory 1989), 34.

9. Richard Exley, *The Rhythm of Life* (Tulsa: Honor Press, 1987), 11.

10. Robert E. Coleman, *One Divine Moment* (Fleming H.

Revell Company), 1970

11. Stephan B. Poulter, *The Father Factor* (Prometheus Books, 2006), 31.

12. Henry B. Biller and Robert J. Trotter, *The Father Factor* (Pocket Books 1994), 214.

13. https://quotefancy.com/quote/1603561/David-Lloyd-Jones

14. https://stories4homilies.wordpress.com/?s=who+is+your+daddy

15. A.W. Tozer, *The Knowledge of the Holy*, (Harper and Row. 1961), 12.

16. Ibid., 112,113.

17. Ibid., 88.

18. J.I. Packer, *Knowing God* (Illinois: InterVarsity Press 1973), 29.

19. Rothman Lily, "*Is God Dead?*", *Time*, April 8, 1966, Vol.87 NO. 14.

20. *Jones, American Man*, 24.

Printed in the USA
CPSIA information can be obtained
at www.ICGtesting.com
LVHW021503081124
796013LV00008B/140